INTERNET

in easy steps

GEOFF PRESTON

COMPUTER STEP

In easy steps is an imprint of Computer Step
Southfield Road . Southam
Warwickshire CV47 0FB . England

http://www.ineasysteps.com

Notice of Liability
Every effort has been made to ensure that this book contains accurate and current information. However, Computer Step and the author shall not be liable for any loss or damage suffered by readers as a result of any information contained herein.

Trademarks
All trademarks are acknowledged as belonging to their respective companies.

Printed and bound in the United Kingdom

ISBN 1-84078-191-2

Contents

Introduction

This chapter introduces the Internet and describes the level of detail that this book goes into.

Covers

Chapter One

Who should read this book?

If you're standing in a bookshop reading this introduction and trying to find out if this is really the book you want, here are a couple of pointers which should make the task a little easier.

Do you want to know about SMTP, POP3 and TCP/IP protocols? If the answer is 'yes', then close the book, put it back on the shelf and look elsewhere. *Internet in easy steps* will be of no use to you whatsoever.

This book is not for techno-freaks.

If, on the other hand, you want to know how to use the Internet effectively and how to make the most of its services, and indeed find out what services are available, then look no further. This is probably the book you need.

What is the Internet?

The name 'Internet' is a very appropriate title: an INTERnational NETwork of computers containing a huge fount of knowledge which anyone with a computer and a telephone line can access.

Internet statistics are mind-boggling. One estimate suggests that the amount of material on the Net doubles every couple of months. Another claim is that every few seconds another individual from somewhere in the world becomes an Internet subscriber. Of the hundreds of websites that are added daily, some are quickly forgotten about, but many thrive.

This indeed is the information super-highway but just as anyone can search the Internet for the information they require, so too can anyone contribute to the global resource of knowledge. Free speech now takes on a whole new meaning. Anyone can put anything on the Internet which can then be accessed worldwide. Pornography, anarchistic philosophies, riot incitement, explosives manufacture – you name it, it's sure to be there. Even sites which do not contain material of this type vary in quality enormously.

But that is the appeal of the Internet.

Servers owned and managed by organisations (Internet Service Providers) are linked by an assortment of cables owned by others e.g. telephone companies, and anyone with a computer can dial into the network and access information held on it.

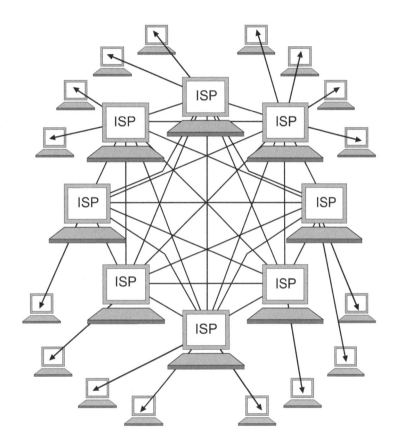

The connection between the end user's computer and the ISP's server need only be a local phone call away, yet the user can access information from the other side of the world which may be routed through more than one server.

How did it start?

Surprisingly the origins of what we now call the Internet date back to the early 1960's and like so much of our modern micro-electronics, its roots lie in war, not peace.

During the late fifties the Cold War was at its height and America and Russia wanted to know what each other was doing. The US Defence Department formed ARPA – the Advanced Research Projects Administration.

The Internet's roots lie in war, not peace.

ARPA recognised that an information system comprising a central super-computer controlling a network of smaller computers would soon become top of the enemy's list of strategic targets. And if it were destroyed, the entire system would fail. ARPA conceived and developed an information network which could not be felled in a single blow. Their solution was not to have a central server but to spread the control over several servers so that whichever servers were knocked out by the enemy, the rest of the system would continue to function. Essentially ARPAnet, as it was termed, was the first decentralized computer network and it evolved into what we now call the Internet.

For more information on ARPAnet, visit: *www.dei.isep.ipp.pt/docs/arpa.html*

Controlling bodies

The key feature of the Internet is that it doesn't have a core. Just as ARPA conceived a decentralised network to prevent the enemy attacking the key element of the system, we have inherited that legacy and what has stemmed from that is the fact that nobody is in overall charge of the Internet. There are millions of people all over the world who are in charge of their little bit, but their jurisdiction doesn't go beyond their front door. And if anyone decides to close down their bit, hardly anyone will notice the difference.

This, it transpires, is both the Internet's strength and its weakness.

As nobody is in overall charge, it is difficult to apply any legislation to control it or regulate it or determine what information is held on it.

The Internet Society was formed to try to establish and maintain common standards. After this came the Internet Network Information Centre (which registers domain names) and the World Wide Web Consortium which tries to establish future developments, in particular programming languages.

These are the only widely recognised bodies who have any say in how the Internet is run and how it is developed. They are the nearest there is to a central authority, but in reality, nobody has the last word.

For a full history of the Internet including ARPAnet, there is an excellent timeline at: *www.pbs.org/internet/timeline/*

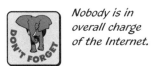

Nobody is in overall charge of the Internet.

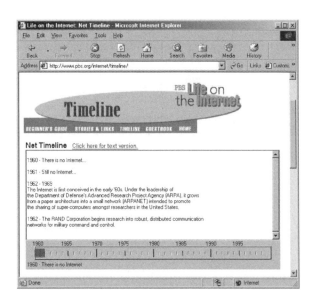

Anyone can join the Internet in almost any capacity. Anyone can send messages over the Internet and anyone can publish whatever they want on the World Wide Web. Individuals can even set themselves up as Internet Service Providers, if they have enough financial clout and a modicum of technical knowledge.

Press coverage on the Internet has alternated between hype and hysteria. All the negative features (of which there are several) are reported on over and over again.

Pornography is high on the list, and seems to attract the most consistent coverage. Yet pornography has been available a lot longer than the Internet.

Sites which incite racial hatred have also had their fair share of airtime. There's not much that can be done about them, but if you disagree with their content, don't visit them. If you're worried that you might accidentally stumble across them, don't be. It does happen that people accidentally find themselves in an undesirable site, but it is very infrequent.

Don't get too bogged down with the negative aspects of the web.

The question of illegal material is a difficult one because what is illegal in one country might not be in another. If you think you're likely to be offended, don't go there.

Sites which provoke public disquiet also feature in the news quite regularly, although not always directly. A recent car cruise in Slough, England was publicised over the Internet. Young drivers with high performance cars gathered to race and show-off on the public roads. What they didn't take into account was the fact that the Police also have access to the same Internet resources and so over 90 officers turned up to greet them.

Stories are now coming to light about drug dealers emailing school children. Doubtless there are other stories in the background waiting to surface.

So why should anyone want to be associated with this filth and degradation?

It is important to balance the negative aspects with the undoubted benefits. People should be aware of the pitfalls and take appropriate measures to protect themselves and enjoy the Internet for what it is – a learning resource, which can and should be enjoyed by everyone.

What do you need?

This chapter outlines what you will require to get connected and offers some alternatives to get you online as painlessly as possible.

Covers

Chapter Two

The hi-tech shopping list

There is more than one method of getting connected to the Internet and the alternative methods are outlined in Chapter 12 on page 172. The most common method of Internet connection is still using a standard telephone line, and this is the method assumed throughout this book.

To get yourself connected to the Internet, you need the following:

- a computer

- a modem

- a phone line

- an Internet account

- a browser

The computer

Although theoretically almost any computer will do, in practice you need a reasonably fast one, especially if you want to be able to use all the multimedia bits. Modern websites contain all manner of goodies such as sound, graphics and even animations and video clips, so you need a computer which will be able to download and run these.

The easiest way to increase the speed of a PC is usually to add more memory.

The current minimum specification is a computer with 32Mb (megabytes) of memory and at least a Pentium 1 processor or equivalent, although if you are buying a computer now you should look for at least 64Mb of memory (to enable you to do things other than use the Internet) and you'll probably now only be able to buy Pentium III or later.

You also need a good screen, certainly one capable of supporting SVGA graphics. Most ready-built computer systems will be supplied with a 15" screen but if you can afford it, and have the space for it, 17" monitors are becoming more widely available.

The latest generation monitors are TFT screens similar to those used on laptop computers. They offer numerous benefits including virtually no flicker, high resolution and no radiation. They also don't attract the dust like conventional cathode ray tube (CRT) monitors.

If you suffer from headaches, a TFT screen might be beneficial.

A TFT monitor like this 15" model, is not essential but worth considering if you spend a lot of time at the computer.

The downside is that, although they are getting cheaper, TFT monitors are still at least 4 times the cost of a CRT monitor of equivalent size.

You'll also need a keyboard and mouse (or equivalent pointing device) which means you'll need an operating system which supports a mouse. That means you'll need a PC running Windows 95, or preferably Windows 98 or later. Older versions of Windows (3.1 or Windows for Workgroups) will work, but you would be well advised to upgrade. All Apple Mac computers qualify, although you should use at least System 7, and preferably a later operating system.

Always try to upgrade to the latest operating system.

To install the software you'll probably need a CD ROM drive as most providers distribute their software on CD ROM. You'll also need some hard disc space to store the software.

The modem

A MOdulator DEModulator is a device that converts the digital signals generated by a computer into analogue signals that can be sent down a standard analogue phone line. It also converts the incoming analogue signals to digital signals that can be read by the computer.

For desktop computers opinion is divided as to whether an internal modem is better or worse than an external modem. For what it's worth, an external modem requires a mains socket to provide it with power whereas an internal modem collects its power from within the computer. With all the other bits and pieces you've got to plug into the mains, the introduction of a mains-powered modem might be one too many.

Fitting an internal modem is not difficult, but if you're unsure, seek professional help.

Internal modems like this model are now routinely fitted to new PCs. If your computer doesn't have a modem, they can be purchased relatively cheaply and fitted easily.

The external modem will also have to be plugged into the computer and frequently the sockets on the back of many computers are in short supply. Internal modems, on the other hand, require an internal connection and these are usually in even shorter supply.

External modems provide a nice array of pretty lights to tell you what they're doing, but the case usually looks unsightly (one was once described as looking like a cheap domestic intercom) and it takes up desk space, which may also be at a premium.

What is certain though is that you should try to get the fastest model you can and at present that is a 56K modem. It may also be advertised as being V90 or V92 standard and will provide noticeably faster access than anything else.

The phone line

Don't have the phone lead trailing across the floor. Always take it around the edge of a room.

For the desktop computer with a modem, you'll need a BT type phone socket near to the computer or a long phone extension lead to connect the modem to the phone line. Kits are available that enable individuals to add a socket to an existing phone installation without having to open the phone sockets.

When you are connected to the Internet (online) you are being charged for the call. If you've selected a good Internet Service Provider it will be a local call, but there will be a charge for the call time unless your phone company makes special provisions for going online. The other point to note is that whilst you're online, the phone is in use. This means that no one can make a call from the phone, and anyone calling you will find the line is engaged.

The cheapest solution to part of this problem is to ask your phone company to provide you with an answerphone service that enables callers to leave messages if your line is engaged. But to really overcome this problem (if indeed it is a problem) a second phone line is required. Many phone companies offer very attractive deals for second lines.

A second phone line is worth considering if you intend spending a long time using the Internet

Most phone lines are analogue but digital lines are becoming more common in homes. The price for installing and maintaining an ISDN (Integrated Services Digital Network) line is now much more affordable, and is getting cheaper. The advantage of a digital line is very much faster Internet access, as well as the ability to handle more than one call at a time. Digital lines are discussed in Chapter 12 on page 172.

Internet accounts

A few years ago, there were relatively few providers. All of them charged their clients per month and some imposed monthly time limitations. Today there are many more ISPs from some very unlikely sources. Many are free.

When choosing an Internet Service provider you should consider these points:

Questions and answers

1.   How much does the connection cost per month?

It varies, but can cost as little as nothing. Don't write off a provider who charges just because they charge, although not all free service providers offer the quality of those providers who do make a monthly charge. Different providers offer different deals at different prices. You get more or less what you pay for.

2.   How much online time are you allowed before the price goes up?

You should have an account with unlimited access. If the one you're considering doesn't have this feature, leave it and go for another.

3.   Do you connect via a local phone number?

If the connection to the ISP is not via a local phone call (e.g. an 0845 number) you're heading for some very large telephone bills. Discard any ISP which does not use local call connection.

4.   How many people can the ISP support at any one time?

The fewer people an ISP can support, the less chance you have of getting a connection first time.

It is sometimes quite tricky to get hold of this information. Beware of some of the new free services as they often do not have the infrastructure to support huge numbers of people. One famous case occurred quite recently when it came to light that a particular free ISP could only support 1500 people on line at a time. No wonder the system was always busy and nobody could get connected!

Free Internet calls are offered by some ISPs but usually using specific phone connections and at particular times of the week only.

5. How fast is the connection?

Like the previous point, it's not always easy to get the answer and when you do (unlike the previous point) the answer doesn't always mean much. Free ISPs often don't run very fast systems. The result will be slow connections, slow download times, but high phone bills.

6. Are you charged for online Technical support? If so, how much?

This is the downside of many free ISPs. Technical support is usually via a premium rate call which works out very expensive. You only need two 10 minute calls per month (which isn't difficult) and you could have spent as much as the most expensive ISP. On the other hand, if you don't call their helpline ever again, you're in profit. (But then, presumably, you wouldn't be reading this book!)

With free ISPs, beware of the hidden cost – telephone help can be very expensive.

7. Does the ISP agreement include email? If so, how many addresses?

Most do include email, but check on the speed of the email delivery as well. Many ISPs provide more than one email address at no extra charge which means you can have a different address for each member of the family. Be aware though, like the letter box on your front door, all emails fall onto the same 'doormat' regardless of who it is for. Emails don't come in envelopes though, so privacy could be an issue.

Multiple email addresses on the same ISP account usually mean everyone can read everyone else's mail.

8. Do you get space on the ISP's server to publish your own website? If so, how much space and how much will it cost?

Most ISPs offer space to publish your own website. Some of the free services charge for this, whilst the services that charge per month throw this in as part of the deal. Don't be fooled into going for a huge amount of webspace. Most ISPs offer 5Mb which is more than enough to publish even the most comprehensive family website.

These points are, to a large extent, intertwined, but they are worth investigating very carefully.

Create a table if you really want to compare ISPs seriously.

Where do I start looking?

Some of the leading subscription ISPs are:

AOL	—	www.aol.com/
BT Internet	—	www.btinternet.com/
Cable & Wireless	—	www.cwnet.com/
Demon	—	www.demon.net/
Direct Connection	—	www.dircon.net/
Easy Net	—	www.easynet.co.uk/
Global Internet	—	www.global.net.uk/
MSN	—	www.msn.com/
Onyx	—	www.onyxnet.co.uk/
Virgin net	—	www.virgin.com/

Once you've selected an ISP and received the installation disc (which will usually be on CD ROM, although some may offer a choice of floppy disc installation), follow the instructions carefully.

Changing your ISP is not necessarily a problem other than the fact that it will also mean your email address and website address will change.

The software for joining a free ISP is usually provided on CD ROM which can be found at the checkouts of many high street shops. If you are already connected to the Internet, you can also join a free service online. Some of the leading providers are:

- Freeserve

- In 2 Home

- Virgin Net

- Zoom

- btclick

- WH Smith

Browsers

The browser is the program that essentially does two things. Firstly it is the software which enables the user to commute to different websites throughout the world. Secondly, it displays the pages of information from the websites.

In simple terms, the browser decodes documents written in a special language called HTML (Hypertext Markup Language). There was a stage when websites featured phrases like 'best viewed with Netscape Navigator', because the different browsers handled documents in very slightly different ways causing slight differences in detail.

Of all the browsers produced since the Internet first became widely used, two have established themselves as supreme: Internet Explorer and Netscape Navigator (now tied up in the total Internet package called Communicator).

If you specifically want Internet Explorer, use an ISP that provides it.

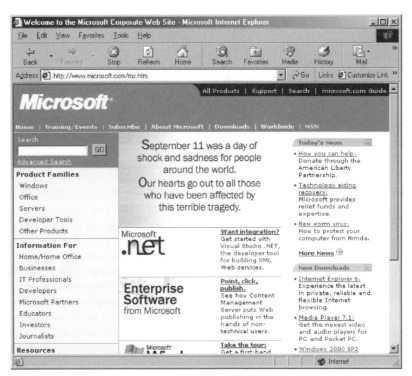

Microsoft's Internet Explorer

Microsoft's Internet Explorer is now just about ahead of Netscape, largely because (some would say) it is supplied free with all versions of Windows. If you've got Windows, you've got Internet Explorer. Further, if you receive a free Internet start-up kit, the chances are it is supplied with Internet Explorer, not Netscape Navigator.

If you specifically want Netscape, use an ISP that provides it.

Netscape Navigator

New versions of both programs come from Microsoft and Netscape at regular intervals. It's usually worth getting the latest version which will invariably contain the latest gizmos.

Both programs can be downloaded from the companies' websites. For Netscape visit *www.netscape.com/* and for Internet Explorer visit *www.microsoft.com/*.

Which browser should I use?

Unless you have decided that you want a particular browser, then it'll probably be best if you stick to the one provided by your chosen Internet Service Provider. Of the discs provided by ISPs for free Internet access, most include Internet Explorer and that will be the browser that will automatically install.

Some 'experts' will try to persuade you that one is better than another, but when they are challenged to provide reasons for their choice, the arguments frequently don't hold water. In fact, in most cases, the explanations provided are based on blind prejudice rather than any logical reasoning.

Views along the lines of 'Anything to do with Bill Gates can't be good' are typical of the explanations forwarded by Netscape followers, whilst Explorer fans will say that there is less chance of their browser conflicting with other Microsoft products.

Stick with the browser supplied by your ISP.

The reality is that there isn't much to choose between either of them. Each time a new version of either package is released it leapfrogs the opposition. So at the moment Explorer may be technically more advanced in some small area, Netscape will then bring out an upgrade that will overtake Explorer, then a new version of Explorer will overtake that and so on.

There are two pieces of advice worth noting when choosing a browser:

1. Whichever browser you choose, make it either Netscape or Explorer unless you really know what you're doing and don't mind being in a minority with a browser that will almost certainly not have had the significant investment of time and money (over a substantial period of time) for its development.

2. Stick with your choice. It's not worth swapping back and forth between them. You can just about run both side by side, but it is not recommended.

Under attack?

Regrettably, there are certain individuals whose sole aim appears to be to spoil your enjoyment of the Internet. Many are particularly gifted people, but prefer to apply their skills destructively rather than for the benefit of the whole Internet community. These are the people who develop viruses.

The more you use the Internet, the more chance you'll have of collecting a virus. Some are fairly harmless and little more than a minor annoyance. Others are vicious and spiteful and can do a great deal of damage to your computer software, including (but not limited to) corrupting or erasing all your work, stealing passwords and other account details and using your email addresses to send incriminating/defamatory/offensive material from your email address to your friends and colleagues.

Use a virus protection program that can automatically download the latest virus definitions so that you are always fully protected against the latest viruses.

Software to protect you from computer virus infection (and virus variants like worms) is a minimum requirement. You should have a good virus protection and cleaning package installed and if you have a permanent connection (see page 172) a firewall to prevent outsiders accessing your work.

One of the most popular is the Norton Antivirus application which can be purchased from most computer suppliers or downloaded from *www.norton.com/*

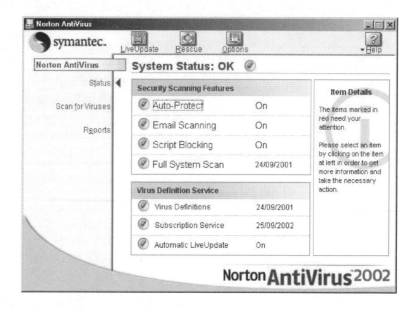

Getting it going

Having got all the bits together, what do you need to do to get it going, and what do you do when it goes wrong? This chapter explains all.

Covers

Chapter Three

Install and connect

It's not easy to give a complete and foolproof description of how to set up the Internet software because currently there are hundreds of ISPs offering different products that each install in slightly different ways. Generally, following the on-screen instructions should work.

If you've activated the Windows Web style feature (Start, Settings, Folder Options), instead of double-clicking (here and elsewhere in this chapter), you should single-click where appropriate.

The example here is using the WH Smith Online disc which is being connected via a standard dial-up connection.

1 Start up your computer and insert the ISP's CD ROM into your CD ROM drive.

2 It should start automatically, but if it doesn't, go to My Computer and double-click on the CD ROM drive (usually Drive D).

3 You should then get the startup logo with some installation options. Choose full installation.

At this point, some ISPs may ask you to complete a registration form which will include your name, address and telephone number, and possibly some other information like the type of computer you're using.

Read the licence agreement carefully.

4 Next comes the licence agreement. Read it and if you agree, click I Accept... and then click Next.

5 You will usually be asked to choose which parts you want to install. It's usually best to stick with Typical. (You can always install other bits later on.) Click Next.

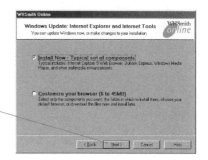

Free Internet CDs are a good way of getting the latest version of your chosen browser.

6 The software will start to install. The blue bar keeps track of its progress. Often there will be a little animated logo which will also help to show that it's all working properly.

7 When the software has finished installing, click on the Finish button and the computer will restart.

This process will have installed the latest version of the browser. Or, to be more accurate, you'll get the version of the browser which is on the installation disc, which will usually be the latest version. If you have a browser already installed, the installation software will only install the browser if it is a later version to the one already installed.

Along with the browser, other software will have been installed. This will vary between different setup discs, but typically you could expect an email program and a web design program.

When the computer restarts, it will continue with the registration procedure. You will then usually get a licence agreement from the service provider. Again, read it carefully and click OK if you agree with it.

It is usually at about this point that the software tries to dial up for the first time. Make sure:

1   The modem is connected to a telephone socket.

2   Nobody else is using the phone in another part of the house/ office.

3   The phone line is actually working.

Someone else on the phone is usually the reason for a failure.

Click the OK button to register and you should get a dial up status box showing that the computer is trying to dial the number:

Some phone companies provide a different dialling tone if you have a message waiting. The alternative tone fools the modem into thinking the line is busy.

When you have successfully connected, you may need to do nothing else, but you may be asked to register your name and address with the ISP.

This will almost certainly be the case if you are using a subscription service, rather than a free service. Typically you will also be given a password with a subscription service.

If you were successful, you should get to your ISP's home page:

If you get a blank page, try typing in the name of a website in the panel at the top.

You will often find a new icon has appeared on the desktop. Double-clicking this will begin the registration procedure. In future you can double-click this icon to get connected.

You'll notice that on the right-hand side of the icon bar (bottom right of the screen) there will be an icon showing two linked computers. The screens will flash from time to time indicating that data is flowing between your computer and that of your ISP. Right-clicking on the icon will open a menu giving you the option to disconnect or open a small window giving details about the connection. The window will give you an indication of the speed of transfer – the higher the better.

What if it goes wrong?

Getting connected to the Internet is not as easy as some would have you believe. It can be an extremely simple task, but it can just as easily be a nightmare.

Troubleshooting

Problems will be either hardware related or software related. Hardware problems are the easiest to sort out so it's often best to start with them.

1.   Is the modem working?

The way to check that the modem and the computer are communicating is to go to Start, Settings, Control Panel and double-click on the modem icon.

Click on the Diagnostics tab and select the modem you are using.

2 Click on More info...

3 If this window comes up blank, the modem is not being recognised by the computer. Clearly this will need to be investigated.

2.   Is the modem actually dialling a number?

This can be checked very easily by turning up the volume of the modem so you can hear what it's doing.

Return to the Control Panel and double-click on Modems.

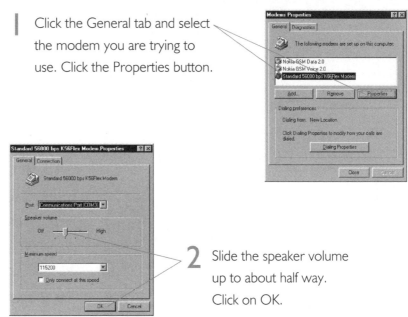

Click the General tab and select the modem you are trying to use. Click the Properties button.

2 Slide the speaker volume up to about half way. Click on OK.

If you lift a telephone receiver you should hear lots of screeching.

This should enable you to hear what's going on. When the computer tries to connect, you should hear the dialling tone, then you should hear the tones as it dials and then you should hear a screeching sound as it tries to communicate with the computer at the other end.

If you don't get any sound output, (and assuming the sound on the computer is working) then check the connection between the modem and the telephone socket. If you do get some sound output, but not as previously described, it's probably because:

- the ISP is engaged

- the computer is trying to dial the wrong number, or;

- other details (e.g. password) are wrong

If it's a free ISP, then an engaged signal is not unusual. Try again later. But the fact that you have got some sound output means that it's not a hardware fault, so you need to look at the setup.

If you've followed the setup procedure, the correct phone number should have been automatically inserted, in which case it's unlikely to be wrong unless the ISP has changed its number (which is not unheard of). To check it, open My Computer, and double-click on Dial Up Networking.

You may also double-click on the file in Dial-Up Networking to connect.

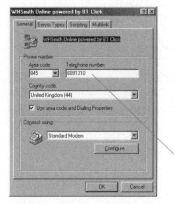

| You should see a file which was created by the installation software. Right-click on it and choose Properties.

2 Check the number is correct. If it isn't, change it and click OK.

Next, try connecting from the Dial-Up Networking file. Right-click on it and choose Connect.

This will open a dialog which should contain the username and password. If the password field is blank, insert your password, click on Save password and then click on Connect.

The computer should try to dial and you'll get a message on the screen telling you that it is dialling:

If you see any of these windows, the computer/software is working. The problem will be with the connection which could be an engaged line or a wrong password.

Once it has communicated with the ISP's computer, it should try to verify your password. A message to this effect will be displayed:

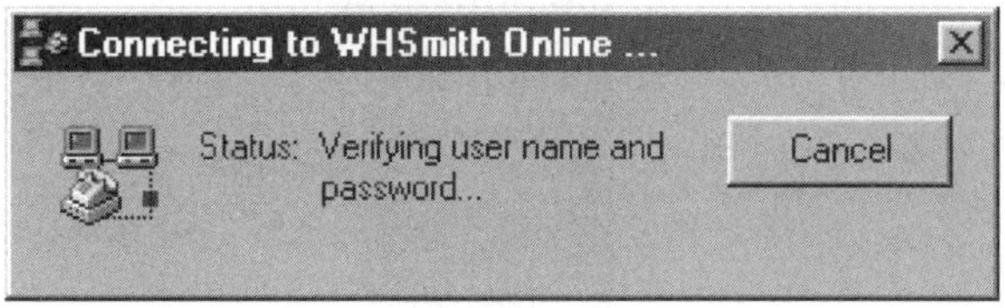

If you've got to this stage, you're almost home because only two things can happen. It can reject your attempt to connect because your logon details are incorrect or it will successfully connect you, in which case you will see:

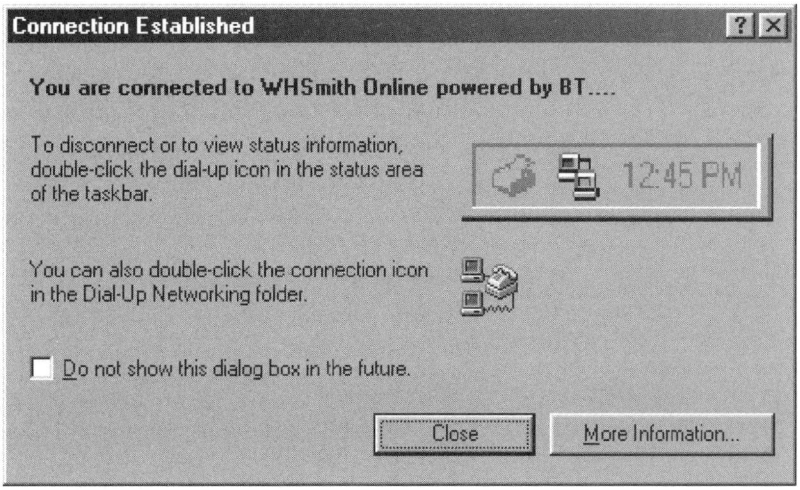

If you get this message, you've succeeded. You're online.

If you've got online by double-clicking the connection file in Dial-Up Networking, you can then start the browser by double-clicking on the browser icon which should be on your desktop.

If launching your browser doesn't get you connected, look at the browser settings.

You should get your ISP's home page. If you don't, but instead get a blank page, try typing in the address of your ISP's site. It will usually be found on the packaging. WH Smith's home page is: *www.whsmith.co.uk/*

Even if you're not using WH Smith as your ISP, typing in this address should still give the same result.

It's ever so slow

The World Wide Wait, as it is sometimes called, can be painfully slow. Getting connected can take an age, but once you are connected, getting to a particular website can take so long that your computer gives up. The possible reasons for this could be:

1.   You're trying to download a page containing huge pictures. Unless you've got a reasonably fast computer and a very fast modem or a broadband connection, some sites are going to be very slow. Website designers generally prefer to use icons for links rather than a simple word which has been entered as text. The benefit is much clearer and slicker sites, but they do take longer to load because a picture, however small it is, uses much more memory than a single word.

2.   The ISP you've chosen isn't very fast or isn't capable of handling the traffic. The problem with some of the smaller ISPs is that they simply do not have the network infrastructure to cope with a high volume of traffic. This problem seems to be particularly noticeable with some of the free providers although it certainly does not apply to all of them.

The Internet is sometimes referred to as the Information Super-Highway. If this is the case, some ISPs appear to be connected via a bridle path.

3.   The rest of the world is also online. There's not a lot you can do about that other than to try again later. Some people will tell you that the afternoon in the UK is slower because it's the morning in the US and they are getting out of bed and coming online. Others tell you to avoid lunch times as all the kids in school are trying to connect, or Sunday afternoon because that's when the hobbyists like to try. The fact is, wherever you are in the world there will be groups in other parts either at work or play trying to get online.

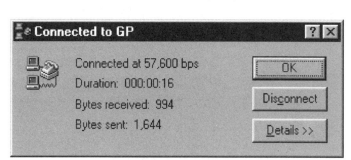

Ping

Another way of checking to see if you have a good connection is to 'ping' another computer. Pinging basically sends a signal to another computer and times its reply. You can ping

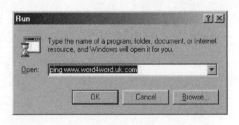

another computer by clicking on Start and choosing Run. In the window, type 'ping' (no quotes) followed by the URL of a known website. If you get a reply you'll see a series of numbers made up from 4 sets of digits separated by full stops. These are IP addresses.

More interesting ping applications are available which give additional information in (usually) a more interesting way. This particular ping program was downloaded from the Internet. There are many similar programs at Tucows (*www.tucows.com*).

The response should be instant.

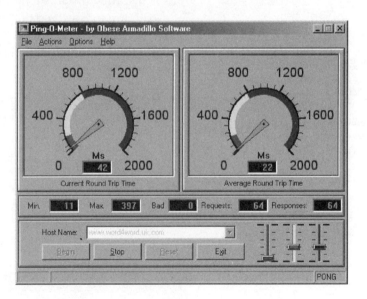

Once the program is running, type in the name of a website and click the Begin button. If it's successful you should immediately get an indication that a connection is live and the speed of the connection.

If you don't get this, but instead get an error message, disconnect and try reconnecting.

The World Wide Web

This chapter introduces you to the World Wide Web, a massive repository of human knowledge. It shows you how to surf the Net, how to find what you're looking for, and how to avoid what you're not looking for.

Covers

Chapter Four

WWW overview

It's remarkable what a catchy name will do. Call it a publications bank (which is effectively what it is) and nobody is interested. Slap on the snazzy tag of World Wide Web, and suddenly everyone wants to know about it and be a part of it.

The web is simply a part of the Internet, and probably of no greater importance than some of its other parts. The web is a repository of ideas, jottings, articles, news, research material and general information. Whatever subject you care to name, there is bound to be something about it somewhere on the web. The trick is finding it.

Even the Queen of England and the President of America have websites.

The rise in popularity of the web is quite extraordinary. In the early 90's very few people had heard about it. Ten years on and anyone who is anyone not only uses it, but has their own website.

Websites can be published by anyone from the largest corporation to the humblest individual. For example, every car manufacturer worldwide has a website and alongside that school children have their own sites. People publish webpages about their hobbies in the hope that others with similar interests will get in touch. Families have websites, which is a great relief as they seem to have taken over from those endless evenings viewing the neighbours' holiday snaps.

Companies have sprung up specialising in web design and production. In fact one of the most startling features is the web's standardisation. Once you have a browser, you can view any web document from anywhere in the world.

This is a testament to the original conception and design of the Internet – it was more or less correct at the start and because it wasn't driven by profit, there weren't dozens of competitors all trying to get their product in-front.

Getting started

Once you have set up your Internet account, run the browser which will connect you to the web and will display a home page.

Initially the home page will almost certainly be that of your Internet Service Provider who takes every opportunity to advertise, especially if it is a free service.

Freeserve's Home Page is a particularly good example of an ISP's home page, but you don't have to start each Internet session with the page that your ISP decides upon.

To change the home page in Explorer, first go to the new page you wish to display as the opening page. From the menu, click on Tools and choose Internet options from the menu. Click on the General tab and click on the Use Current button. In Navigator, click on Edit and choose Preferences from the menu. Choose Navigator in the left panel and click on the Use Current Page button. Then click OK.

How to work the web

The philosophy behind the World Wide Web is simple – use key words in a document to link to other documents. In other words, hypertext. This was the original idea of Tim Berners-Lee, a physicist working at the European Particle Physics Laboratory in Geneva.

On the WWW, the hypertext links can connect documents which may be on different computers and even in different parts of the world. As a user, you don't usually know precisely where the information resides, and you don't need to. It's all quite seamless and painless. That is until you find that the rest of the world is also trying to use the Internet and then it can be very slow (i.e. slow to the point that you think it's stopped working).

Look for the links to other pages, but don't forget the 'back' and 'forward' arrows on the browser's button bar.

How do I recognise a link?

Unless specified otherwise, hypertext links will show up as underlined text, usually in a different colour from the rest of the text. Clicking on the link will take you to another document which should in some way be related to the link you selected.

But it is not just words that can be links. Pictures, tables and diagrams too can be linked to other documents. The pictures can be small icons or logos, or full colour photographs. For this reason, the links have become known as hyperlinks.

Sometimes graphics do not show any obvious signs that they are links. This is because (for example) a thick blue line around an icon would spoil its appearance. But all links reveal themselves when the mouse is moved over them because the mouse pointer changes from a pointer to a hand. The three most common pointers are:

⌶   over a piece of copyable text

☝   over a hyperlink

⬀   over nothing in particular

Consider this page from a well-known website:

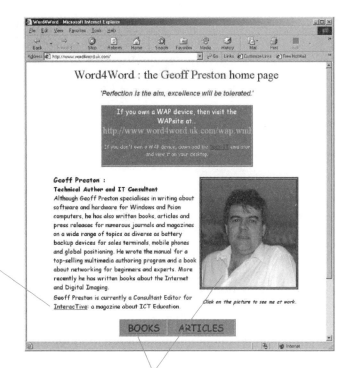

Hyperlink

You won't always know if a link takes you to another page on the same site, or another site.

Both the underlined text and the picture are hyperlinks. Clicking the left mouse button when the pointer is over the BOOKS link opens...

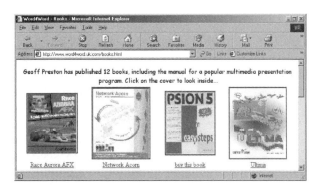

... another page on the same site (rather like opening a new page in the same book). But clicking on the hyperlink flagged in the top screenshot...

Back arrow

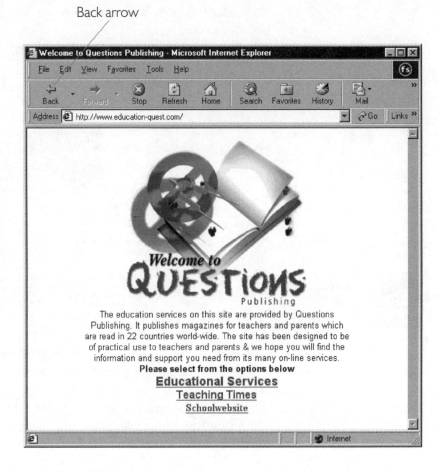

... opens a web page which is stored on a different computer in another part of the country. In fact, this page could have been stored on a computer in another part of the world.

Once here, there may be links to other sites in other parts of the world.

Don't forget to use the arrow at the top of the browser to backtrack through the sites you visited en route to your destination.

How do I start surfing?

There are several ways to get going, but one of the most straightforward ways is to type in the name of a site in the panel at the top of the browser. The problem with this method is that you have to copy the address exactly as it is written, including punctuation, as one missed full stop will ensure that it won't work.

You can get website addresses from a variety of places. Inclusion of a web address is now almost obligatory in many forms of advertising, letterheads and business cards.

Once you arrive at a website, there will often be hyperlinks to take you to other related sites. Sometimes the relationship is a little tenuous, but that's the diversity of the web.

In most cases the address will begin:

You don't have to enter http:// as most browsers insert it automatically.

http://www.

This will be followed by the domain name of the site, which could be the name of a company or individual followed by either *com* or the type of Internet account followed by the country. To be strictly accurate, this would be followed by a forward slash (/) but this can be ignored when typing the address.

Additional slashes followed by other words at the end of an address indicates a page on the website. Therefore:

http://www.freeserve.co.uk/services

The second part of this book gives some interesting websites with full descriptions.

means that *services* is a page of the *Freeserve* site and typing in that address in full will take you directly to that page rather than going to *Freeserve*'s home page and navigating to the *service* page from there.

Sifting through the web

The sheer size of the web is beyond human comprehension. If you want to find a piece of information, or you want to visit a specific site, it is unrealistic to embark on a trawling expedition in the hope that you might stumble across what you want.

You need to organise a search, and for that you need some specialist tools to help you search. Thankfully there are several, and most are free.

There are two main types of search tool that you need to know about in order to find the information you want.

Indexed websites

It's worth making a search engine or directory your home page.

Sometimes referred to as a directory, this type of site has been 'hand-built' and contains a hierarchical index. This simply means that a number of subjects are listed as an index. Clicking on one of the subjects takes you to another index listing topics within that subject. Clicking one of those takes you to yet another index of topics. Eventually you should arrive at a list of sites which focus on the very specific subject you're researching.

It's important to remember that indexed sites have been put together by humans and so humans are required to update and amend them. As a result, some of these sites are not always as up-to-date or accurate as one might like.

Search engines

A search engine requires you to enter a word, a group of words or a phrase and the computer (theirs, not yours) will perform a search for that word or phrase. It can search a huge number of pages very rapidly and will (or at least should) return a list of sites that specifically relate to the text you entered.

The trick here is to learn how to enter the word or group of words so that you hit just a few sites, one or more of which, hopefully, will provide you with what you want to know.

Searching by subject

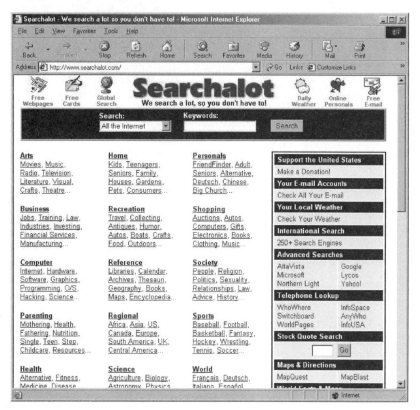

The object of any search is to progressively sift out unwanted material.

Searchalot is typical of a number of index sites that can be used to track down information. The advantage of sites such as this is that you can locate the information you need by simply clicking the hyperlinks. The disadvantage is that it will only take you to the home page of each website.

The opening page shows a range of subjects conveniently divided into categories. Every underlined word is a hyperlink so it should be possible to find some information about a subject just by clicking the links.

Each time you click a hypertext link, you'll be taken to another page which only contains links within the subject category requested.

Let's say we want to find some information about Origami (paper folding) and in particular, paper aeroplanes.

Origami is undoubtedly a craft, and in the Art category is a hyperlink called Crafts. Clicking that link opens...

...the 'Arts: Crafts' page containing links to 5170 sites! Among the topics is 'Origami', and there are links to 98 sites.

Clicking on the 'Origami' link...

... opens the 'Arts: Crafts: Origami' page with 24 links to sites about paper aeroplanes.

Clicking on this link...

... opens the page which lists the 24 sites about paper aeroplanes. 'Ken Blackburn's Paper Airplane Page' looks interesting, so click this:

and up comes a website about paper aeroplanes. On the left is a hyperlink to instructions for making a paper plane. Click on this link...

Back arrow

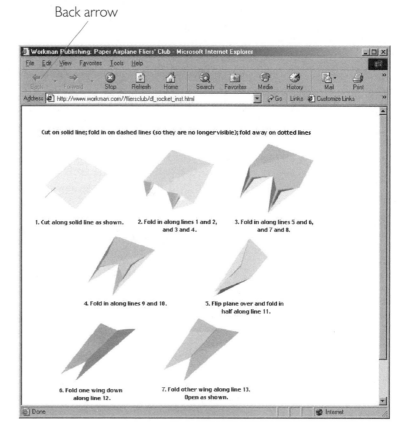

When you get to a site that you think you might like to visit again, save it in Favorites.

... and up come details of the record-breaking plane which you can recreate with the instructions provided in the comfort of your own home.

The flagged arrow at the top of the screen (shown here on Netscape's browser) will take you back to the pages previously visited. This means you can easily backtrack to, say, the page containing the list of paper aeroplane sites and visit another.

A word of caution

Remember, index sites have been constructed by humans and are not necessarily totally accurate. Just because a site is not found using one of these tools doesn't mean it doesn't exist.

Searching by keyword

Another way of searching the web is to enter a keyword into a search engine.

Search engines work in a different way to an index or directory as the computer tries to match a word or group of words which the user has entered (known as a keyword). The match can be not only against a title of a web document, but also occurrences of the keywords within the document itself.

There are several search engines which can be accessed either by going to the website of a search engine or by going to another website that uses one of the search engines.

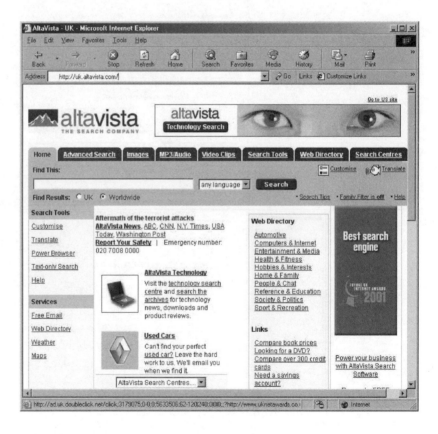

AltaVista is about the largest search engine and can carry out both simple and complex searches very rapidly.

Simple searches

A simple search requires that the user enter a keyword. Continuing on the theme of paper aeroplanes, let's see if there is another way of tracking down the information we're looking for.

AltaVista's home page is at: *www.altavista.com/*

1 The first task when setting up a search is to choose the language: retrieving unreadable information is pointless. Click on the arrow and choose a language from the menu.

2 Enter keywords in the panel. AltaVista is a particularly efficient search engine which will allow you to enter questions and meaningful phrases as well as a single word. Enter the words *paper aeroplane* and click on Search.

In a few seconds (or minutes depending on the time of day and the speed of your hardware) you'll get the results:

7276 articles are returned, which is rather a lot, although entering just *paper* or *aeroplane* probably would have resulted in millions of sites.

Clicking on the hyperlinks (underlined) takes you to the sites.

But that is a lot of sites to trawl through so you'll need to narrow it down a little, so that you get fewer results.

The easiest way to do this is to restrict the amount of the web that is being searched.

Below the AltaVista toolbar is a row of six buttons. Clicking one of these will search only in that area of the web.

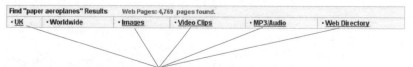

Click on one of these buttons (whilst keeping the rest of the search setup the same) will narrow down the search significantly. For example, clicking on the UK tab will return:

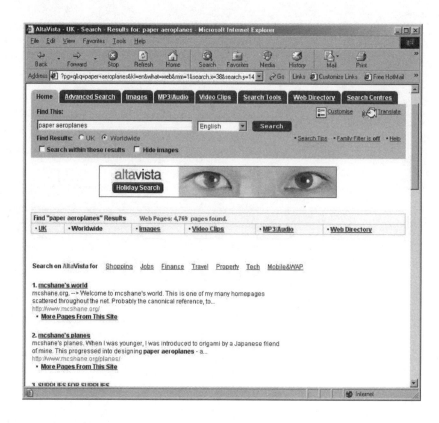

This restricted search delivers fewer sites which can then be searched manually by clicking on the hyperlinks. Clicking on one of the links on the search page opens a site relating to paper aeroplanes:

You may find some sites listed that apparently have no connection with your search.

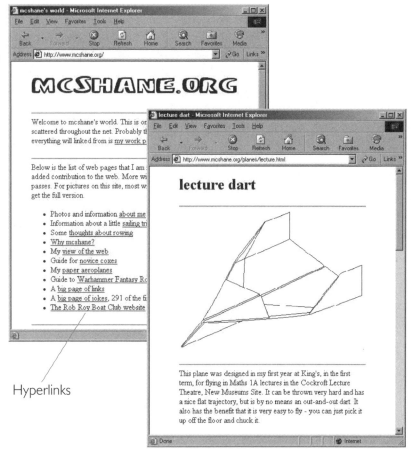

Hyperlinks

Clicking on the hyperlinks on the home page will take you to the pages you want to view within the site.

Another way to narrow down a simple search is to choose one of the other tabs. Images is often a useful one to use.

Advanced searches

The problem with a simple search is that it often achieves so many matches or hits that you're still left with 1000's of sites to wade through to get the information you want.

Advanced Search tab

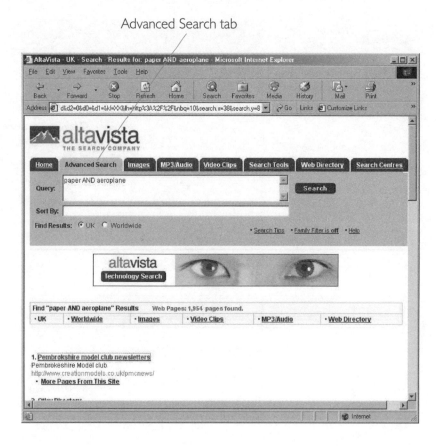

From the AltaVista home page, clicking on the Advanced Search tab opens a page with much more sophisticated searching facilities which should return fewer hits, if you enter the parameters correctly.

When setting up an advanced search, you can enter some additional words which determine how the search engine will treat the keywords you entered. There are about half-a-dozen of these words (known as Boolean operators after George Boole who spent many years studying mathematical logic).

Of the various operators which the search engines understand, the two most important are AND and OR:

paper AND aeroplane

Entering this search will return articles which contain both *paper* and *aeroplane*. Documents that only contain *paper* or only contain *aeroplane* will be ignored.

This is used when you want to search for two subjects that are linked, as is the case here.

paper OR aeroplane

This search will return all documents that contain the words *paper* and *aeroplane*, just as in the previous example. But it will also return all documents which just contain the word *paper* as well as those documents which just contain the word *aeroplane*.

This would be used when (for example) you don't have a preference about spelling. You could use OR if you didn't know whether to search for *aeroplane* or *aeroplanes*.

These operators can be used together to form quite complex statements. Brackets can also be included and these will be calculated first.

paper AND (aeroplane OR aeroplanes)

This expression would search for either spelling of aeroplane and paper. In other words:

paper and *aeroplane*, *paper* and *aeroplanes*, but not *paper* on its own, *aeroplane* on its own or *aeroplanes* on its own.

This is quite different from:

(paper AND aeroplane) OR aeroplanes

This expression (or one similar) would almost certainly be a mistake. It would return documents containing *paper* and *aeroplane* together with all documents containing the word *aeroplanes* on its own.

Once the search expression has been entered, there are some other options which should help to narrow down the results.

Ticking One result per web site will help reduce the number of 'hits' on a single site.

As with simple searches, entering the language will remove a large number of documents that you can't read.

If you know the date the document was originally published (or two dates between which the document was published) then you can enter the dates, and documents falling outside those dates will be ignored.

Finding the engines

Experience has shown that rather than needing one search engine, you'll soon find yourself using several. Different search engines frequently give different results for a particular search.

Searchalot provides a simple way of accessing several Internet search engines, enabling you to carry out lots of different searches from the same place.

To select the search engine you wish to use, click on the arrow to the right of the panel headed Search:

A menu will open (of which this is just a part) listing several search engines. Click on the one you wish to use and its name will appear in the panel.

Now enter a keyword in the panel on the right, and click the Search button to begin the search.

Advanced searches using most search engines can be carried out directly from the Searchalot site, and from many other similar sites.

The Ask Jeeves site is a very popular and graphically pleasing search site. Usually choosing to search from a single search engine like Ask Jeeves, will return a more manageable selection of results.

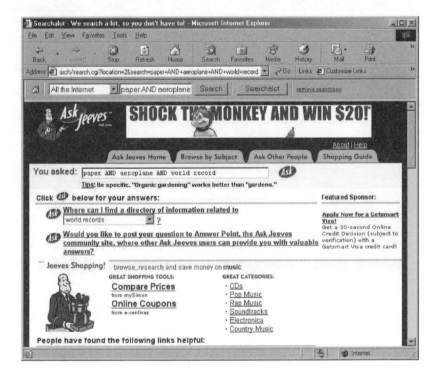

Specialist searching

There are sites which offer very specific search facilities within a specific topic. If you want to search for books or music, for example, Amazon is probably the best place to visit.

When you arrive at the site you can look at stories and articles which can be accessed by clicking the hyperlinks or you can perform a search for a specific book.

| Choose a book or music from the list

2 Enter a keyword which can be title, publisher or author

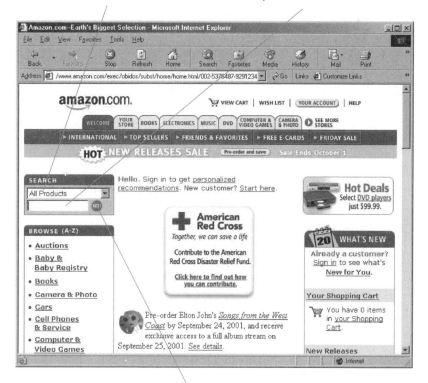

3 Click Go

Amazon allows you to enter either the name of an author, the name of a book or a book's ISBN.

Entering *longitude* displays the books with 'longitude' in the title, but also displays other books which might be on the same or similar subjects.

This is a simple search facility which can generate a large list of books. If you know the name of the author you can enter it but it will not necessarily list only the books by the author you chose. It almost certainly will list some books by authors with a similar name.

Clicking on the name of the author will search for other books by the same author. Again, it's searching for a particular word. Any other author with the same name will also be included in the final list.

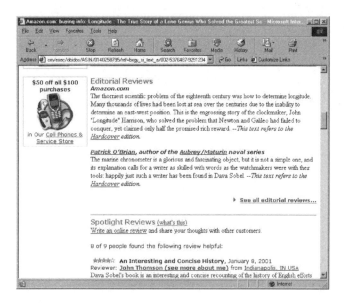

Look out for special offers like signed copies of books.

Clicking on the name of a book will display information about that particular book – usually in the form of a third party review, or as above, two third party reviews.

Clicking on the name of a book will again display information about the book, frequently with a picture of the cover:

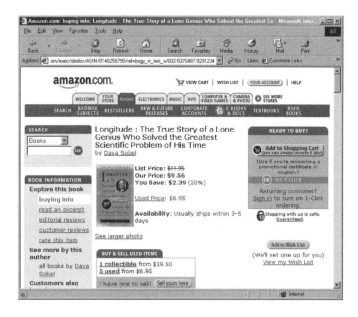

Yellow Pages

Now you don't have to 'let your fingers do the walking' because Yellow Pages are on the web and the online version is far, far easier to use than the book version.

Go to the Yellow Pages home page at *www.yell.co.uk/* or *www.yell.com/* and to start a search do the following:

1 Enter either the type of service or the name of a company or tradesman.

2 Enter the area, which can be either a place or a postcode, and click Search.

This is far easier than using the book version.

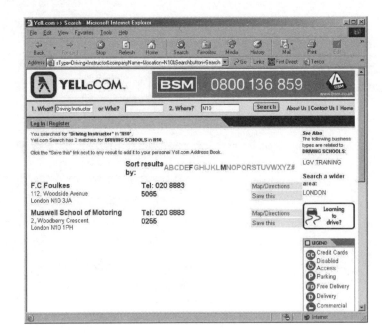

The results come back very quickly and, as can be seen, there are two driving instructors in the N10 area. If the map icon appears alongside, clicking on it will display a map giving directions of how to get there.

The input panel is displayed, ready for a new search.

Webrings

Searching for a specific subject on the web is not always easy and searching for several sites on the same subject can sometimes be laborious. A clever way of accessing several websites on the same subject is to go to a webring.

Use your browser's 'Favorites' feature to store useful pages from the ring.

A webring is a group of websites linked to each other in a sort of circle.

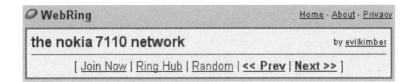

On each webring website are links to take you either forward or back around the webring. If you keep going in one direction you'll eventually get back to where you started.

Finding a ring

There are two ways to find a webring. The first is to go to the index and choose from the list (categorised by subjects) and then choosing topics within those subjects. Clicking on the hyperlinks will eventually take you to a site on that ring.

There is a webring for just about every subject imaginable.

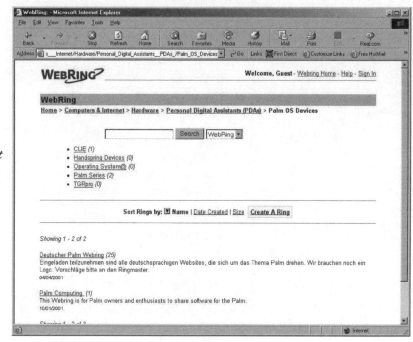

Each link has a brief description of the subject of the webring which should help you choose the one you want.

The other way to find a ring on a specific topic is to use the webring database search. Typing in a word or phrase will list all the rings on that topic.

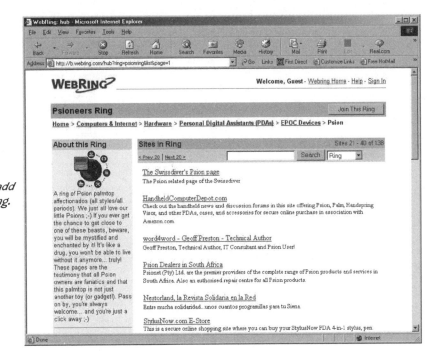

Anyone can add a site to a ring.

Entering the keyword *Psion* results in a dozen rings about various aspects of Psion computers. Clicking on one of the rings (*Psioneer*) reveals over 130 sites in this ring alone!

The list of sites is displayed and clicking on one of the hyperlinks takes you to that particular site. Once there, the first thing to do is find the ring icon so that you can navigate around the ring.

Anyone can add their own website to a webring and details of how to do this may be found on the Webring home page.

There are hundreds of webrings on a huge variety of topics ranging from the obscure to the widely popular which can be accessed from *dir.webring.com/*

Protecting yourself

The Internet is a great tool for kids to learn from. But it does contain some areas that you may not wish your child to visit, and indeed might not want to visit yourself.

The responsibility, in this instance, is firmly with parents. It is wholly inappropriate to buy the kids a computer, install it in their bedroom and then abdicate all responsibility for it. The computer needs to be in a place where its use can be monitored.

Monitoring can be carried out in two ways. First, the occasional glance at the screen. If the screen is in view of parents when a child is using the computer, then all it takes is a quick glance occasionally. In fact, not even a glance is required because if the children know that what is on the screen can be seen by mum and dad, then clearly they're not going to go in search of unsuitable material.

The second method is slightly more devious. Go to the browser and click on the History button. This will list all the sites visited over a given period:

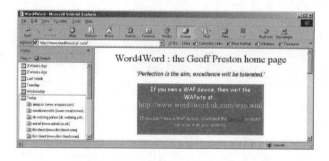

Favorites can be deleted so it's not an absolute check.

You can also get to this list by going to My Documents and clicking on drive C. Open the folder called Windows and inside will be a folder called History. Inside are folders containing the sites visited over a period of time.

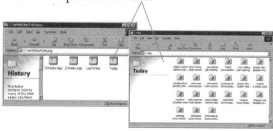

Software monitoring

Parental monitoring is fine provided you are able to monitor the computer's use on a 24 hour basis. Clearly this is not always possible and so you might want to invest in some software protection which will also trap sites found accidentally, and may even limit Internet access.

Net Nanny is one of a number of software tools that will allow parents to control their children's Internet activity by preventing the display of sexually explicit material, graphically violent material, material advocating hate groups and material advocating illegal activity, such as drug use, bomb making, or underage drinking and gambling.

GetNetWise

If the kids are using the Internet, a protection program must be regarded as a minimum requirement.

Parents can find out more about protecting themselves and their children by visiting *www.getnetwise.org/*

There are reviews about a wide variety of children-friendly materials including search engines for kids.

Free speech?

Without doubt, there is a great deal of material which many people would describe as undesirable. In some countries, a great deal of this material is illegal.

Should we protect ourselves from material such as this?

Regardless of which country you live in, the chances are you are living in a free country which supports free speech. It means that we as individuals have the right to say what we want (within certain limits).

Overt searches for pornographic material may be seen as acceptable for some, by some. But surely allowing children to accidentally stumble across this type of material is unacceptable?

If you think you're going to be offended, don't visit the site.

Most newspaper shops sell magazines which would be described as soft-porn. They can be found on the top shelf and although the covers explicitly tell of their contents, they are in fact fairly inoffensive in themselves – usually featuring a scantily-clad model which is not much different from what could be seen on any seaside beach. We all know what's inside and if you're likely to be offended, don't open it. This prevents the subject being inflicted on those who do not wish to be part of it, but it's clearly available for those who do. The choice is yours.

In many cases the Internet does not provide that safeguard. Apparently innocent searches can be made but results may include sites of this type which are not presented in a 'plain inoffensive wrapper'. This seems to be forcing the views of one person onto another which is contrary to the principle of free speech.

And what about some of the extreme political parties? Should these be barred? If so, why? Would you want them banned because you personally do not approve of their philosophies? In which case, would you want to ban the websites of any of the mainstream political parties because you also don't approve of their policies?

It's food for thought, nothing more.

Email

This chapter introduces electronic mail and outlines how to use it, and how not to abuse it.

Covers

Chapter Five

What is email?

Of all the features provided by the Internet, this is probably the most widely used.

The world has known about electronic mail (or email) for several years, but it is only relatively recently that it has taken off and become widely known and widely used. Indeed many people would now claim that without email, at best they would be seriously hampered in trying to carry out their daily work and at worst they would simply not be able to function. Frankly I believe the worst-case scenario is a myth – we could function without email, but life is certainly a great deal easier with email than without.

Email is very fast. Send an email and the recipient could get it within seconds, wherever they may be in the world.

The benefits of email are many, but top of the list is probably the fact that recipients can read their mail even if they're away from their desk. The recipient, using any computer in the world (with a phone line attached), can connect to the Internet and any messages will be delivered to the computer that person is currently using, wherever it may be.

Emailed messages will wait until the recipient is ready to collect them. Messages go into the mail box (which is usually at the recipient's Internet Service Provider) until the recipient logs on and it is delivered.

You can be sure that if you send an email to an individual, that individual will get it, providing s/he logs on to collect it.

The other advantage is that machine-readable documents, including (small) computer programs can be attached to emails thus enabling the recipient to amend and print top copies within minutes of the documents being sent.

On the downside, email could all but replace conventional mail with subsequent impact on postal jobs throughout the world. But it is unlikely to completely replace the conventional postal service which can deliver goods as well as the printed word.

Email in action:

You can send email to one person (in which case only that person may be able to read it) or to a group of people.

1 The sender composes a message and connects to his/her service provider. The message is then sent to the ISP's computer.

2 The sender's ISP uses the recipient's email address to pass the message...

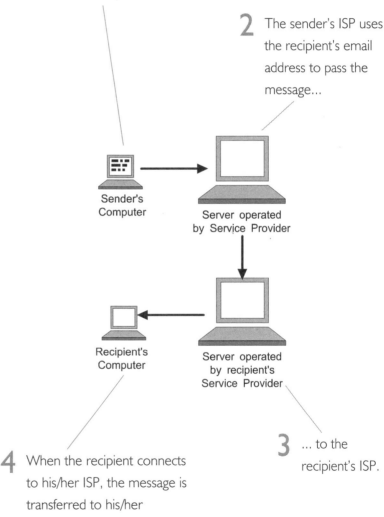

Sender's Computer

Server operated by Service Provider

You may attach a document or documents to an email. For example, you may send a brief message, but attach a ten page, fully formatted MS Word document.

Recipient's Computer

Server operated by recipient's Service Provider

3 ... to the recipient's ISP.

4 When the recipient connects to his/her ISP, the message is transferred to his/her computer.

Email addressing

Just as traditional letters must be correctly addressed, so too must email messages. Email addresses look confusing, but they are really quite straightforward. The basic format of an email address is:

\<user's name\>@\<domain\>.\<account type\>.\<country\>

The user's name is that of the individual and would normally reflect the user's real name. (I have three email accounts: *gp*, *gpreston* and *geoff* which I use for different purposes.)

The domain name is the name of the server or service provider on which the account is held. In some cases, this can be changed so that the domain name reflects the name of your company or even your own name.

After the domain comes the type of account, then the country of origin, unless the previous part is *com*.

Consider the following account name, which is fairly typical:

gp@freeserve.co.uk

Breakdown:

gp	the individual user's name
@	pronounced 'at'
freeserve	the Internet domain
co	indicates a commercial company
uk	indicates the account is held in the UK.

For those still confused, a useful analogy is with a conventional address in a street. The name is rather like the name or number of a house. In general, you can have any name you like as long as nobody else in the street has the same name or number. The Internet domain name is like the name of the street. The country is the same. The analogy breaks down a little with the type of account, but it would be rather like putting 'hotel', 'shop' or 'private residence' in the postal address.

The different types of account you're likely to come across are:

ac	an academic institution
com	a commercial company
co	a commercial company
gov	a government department
org	a non-profit-making organisation
sch	a school

The different countries you're likely to meet are:

at	Austria
au	Australia
ca	Canada
ch	Switzerland
es	Spain
fi	Finland
fr	France
de	Denmark
ie	Ireland
il	Israel
is	Iceland
it	Italy
jp	Japan
kr	Korea
nl	Netherlands
nz	New Zealand
se	Sweden
tw	Taiwan
uk	United Kingdom
za	South Africa

It's worth knowing where email addresses reside if only for an indication as to the language spoken by the recipient.

Email software

Managing emails

In order to compose, send, receive and read emails, it's best to have a dedicated program, although you can often access your emails from your ISP's website.

Dedicated email programs usually offer more comprehensive management of your email. There are several to choose from, including many which are free.

The two most common are:

Outlook Express

Although this is given away, it doesn't mean you are free to make illegal copies, or break the copyright agreement.

This email program is usually installed as part of Microsoft's Internet Explorer and as such it's effectively free. It's probably the most widely used email program as it's also the one that's given with most free Internet CDs.

There are four 'trays' for incoming mail, outgoing mail, old messages you've sent and old messages received.

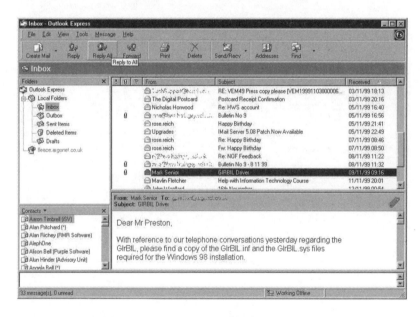

Messages can be easily viewed by clicking on the title of the message (in the top panel) and the contents will be revealed in the lower panel. Double-clicking displays the message in a separate window from where it can be printed.

Netscape Messenger

This comes as part of the Netscape suite and is effectively the head-to-head rival of Outlook Express.

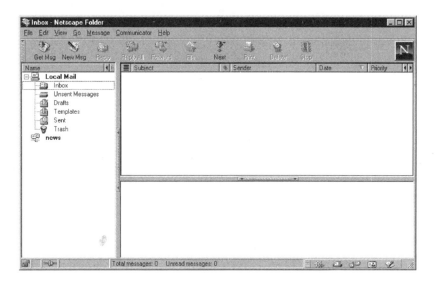

It's not usually worth changing your email program, but it is worth keeping up to date with the latest versions.

The reality is that these two programs are virtually identical (in so far as what they do). In other words, if you've already got one, it's unlikely to be worth your while changing to the other. The additional benefits are unlikely to be worth the hassle of changing.

Others

These are by no means the only email programs available. If you want something different, try Eudora which can be downloaded from:

www.qualcomm.com/

There are two versions, 'lite' which is free, and 'Pro' for which there is a small charge but you get several additional features.

Pegasus is available as a free download from:

www.pmail.com/

This is brilliantly simple to set up and use.

Setting up your email program

Many Internet Service Providers (including all of the free ones) supply a disc which will install and set up most of your email account for you. But whatever ISP and email program you choose to use, you'll need to do some setting up yourself. This actually involves little more than entering a few names in boxes. Most of the details will be provided by your ISP, but some details (those personal to you) may have to be decided upon by you.

Your name – when sending an email, your name (which may be your real name, or the name you wish others to identify you by) will be sent along with your messages so that others will know who the message is from.

Email address – if you have been provided with an email address then this will need to be entered so that recipients will know who to reply to.

Incoming mail server – your ISP will provide you with this name but in most cases (where Internet access is via a single computer connected to a single telephone line) the address will be:

pop.<isp name>.<account type>

Outgoing mail server – again, your ISP will provide you with this name which will usually be:

smtp.<isp name>.<account type>

You will be asked if you want the system to remember your password. If you're the only person using the computer, confirm that you do.

Account name – this will be the name by which the account is registered by the ISP. It may or may not reflect your own name.

Password – this may or may not be provided by the ISP. In any event, when it is entered it will be displayed as a row of asterisks so that nobody else can read it.

News server – you may also be asked to enter the name of the news server. Typically, this will take the form of:

news.<isp name>.<account type>

Outlook Express

To change or view your account details in Outlook Express:

1 Click on Tools. In the pull-down menu, choose Accounts.

If you want to create a new account, click on Add before step 2.

2 Click on the Mail tab and select the account you wish to change.

3 Click on Properties.

4 The details will be under the General and Servers tabs.

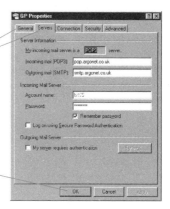

5 Click OK to save any alterations.

Netscape Messenger

When changing your account details in Messenger:

1   Click on Edit, and from the menu choose Preferences.

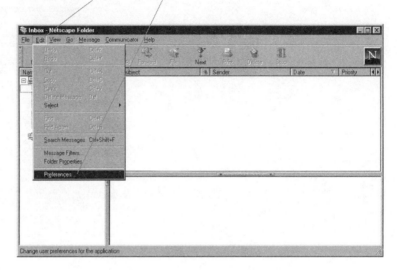

2   Choose Identity and Mailservers to view or alter the account details.

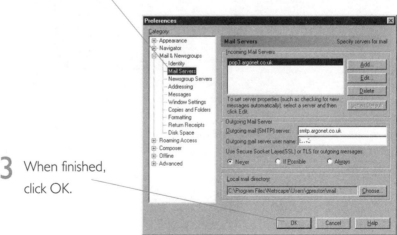

3   When finished, click OK.

Fine-tuning

Most email programs will allow you to set an assortment of options which will control the way the email program works.

From Outlook Express go to Tools and choose Options, from Messenger go to Edit and choose Preferences.

(Outlook Express)

(Netscape Messenger)

You will find the best options for you as you begin using emails on a regular basis, but some of the options you should consider are:

When to connect

You can set your email program to automatically connect as soon as it is started. This means that any new messages will be delivered when you start.

When to disconnect

I can't think of a good reason why you need to stay connected after you've sent and received emails. Set it to automatically log off after send and receive.

Spell-checking

It's worth setting it so that it will spell-check your messages before they are sent. You can also include checking any text written by someone else that is being included in the reply.

Free email accounts

Email need not cost anything, apart from the cost of your ISP and phone calls. If your ISP does not provide a very good email service, or you simply want another email address, try using a free email service like Toast.

Log on to Toast at *www.toast.com/*

If you haven't registered, you'll be asked to provide a username and a password. This can be a little tricky as there are several million account holders worldwide, and so choosing a suitable name that isn't already in use is often harder than one would think.

This is also a way of sending anonymous emails.

Once you are registered, you can go to the Toast site and enter your username and password.

This, of course, can be done from any computer in the world, so you can collect email when you're away from the office and even using someone else's computer.

When you've successfully logged on, you will be presented with a window listing all the emails currently waiting for you.

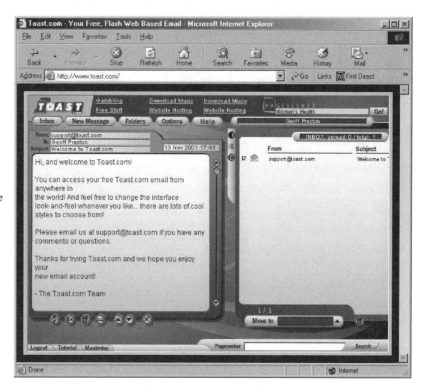

If there are several people in your household who all want private email addresses, use a free email service to provide them.

Those messages which have been read can be saved (to be read again later), printed or deleted. New, unread messages are highlighted enabling you to distinguish new mail from old.

It's far better to compose emails offline.

You can create new messages in Toast although it's sometimes better to prepare messages in a word processor whilst 'offline' and then copy and paste the text into the Toast when you are online. This practice reduces the phone bill very significantly.

Like most email services of this type, Toast is very secure and very fast. The main restriction with many free email services is that you cannot send and receive messages with large attachments like high resolution pictures.

Web email

Accessing emails from your ISP's website

Many Internet Service Providers offer their customers the facility of accessing their emails directly from their website.

BlueYonder is typical of ISPs that allow users access to their emails through the ISP's website. To access your email this way:

This is the best way to access your email if you're trying to do it away from your computer – at an Internet Cafe for example.

1 Go to your ISP's website and look for a link to take you to your email.

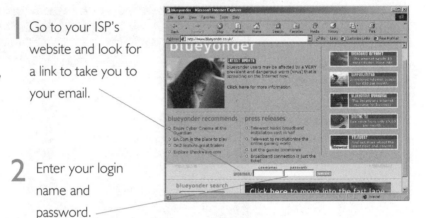

2 Enter your login name and password.

This opens your email account showing what emails you have, which are new and which have been read:

If you're going away but still want to be able to access your emails, remember to take your login name and password with you.

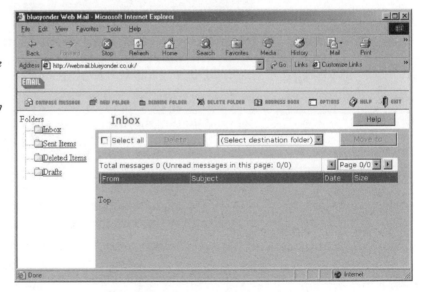

Corporate email

Many companies run an internal mailing system which works in exactly the same way as Internet email, but some mail is kept within the company.

Typical of the many programs used for this is IMail which enables users to send both corporate and Internet email. Users create mailings and, depending on how they are addressed, IMail will determine where they go. A full email address will be sent via the Internet, whereas anything less will be sent internally.

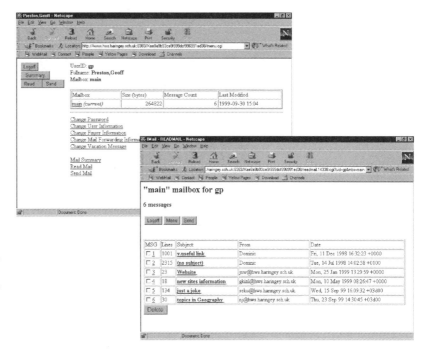

Your loved one might not appreciate you taking your work on holiday.

IMail offers the user several additional features which could prove invaluable. You can tell the system to redirect the mail you usually collect via IMail to another (Internet) email address. This means that you can collect your corporate mail when you're away from the office.

If you're on holiday, you can tell IMail to send an acknowledgement back to anyone who sends you an email telling them you're away and you'll reply when you return.

Anatomy of an email

Address books

The trouble with most email addresses is that they are anything but memorable. Some are little more than an apparently meaningless string of characters – sometimes not even containing letters in the first part.

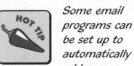

Some email programs can be set up to automatically add names from all incoming and outgoing emails to the address book.

Most popular email programs have an address book which enables you to store the names and addresses of those you frequently contact. Using this system, you can simply enter the person's name in the To box, or even just select it from a list.

The added advantage is that when you look at emails you have previously sent, you can quickly see who you sent them to.

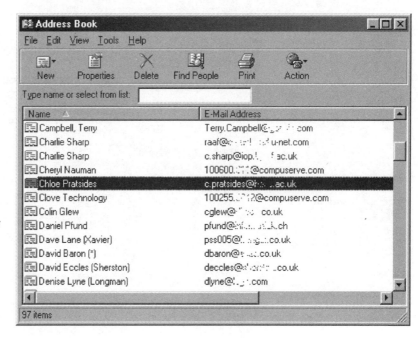

You can also send to several people by creating a list in the To box.

CC and BCC

When you've selected the recipient you may, if you wish, forward the email to one or more people by entering another recipient in the CC or Counter (Carbon) Copy box. If you don't want the recipients to know who else you have sent the message to, you should put the other names in the BCC or Blind Counter (Carbon) Copy box.

Subject

It's worth including a short phrase in the Subject box as it gives the recipient an idea of what the message is about before they open and read it. It is particularly helpful if, like me, you store past emails for reference. If there's a subject, you can quickly scan the messages for the one you want. If you find you've got 20 messages from the same person and none contain an indication of what they are about, it could take a long time to find what you're looking for.

The body of an email

An emailed communication can seem a little curt (rather like a telegram) and some people can be offended by this. It is particularly noticeable if a reply contains huge chunks of the original mailing with just a couple of words added.

A whole new writing style has developed with emails.

To be on the safe side, especially when sending an email to someone for the first time, lay it out a little like a traditional handwritten letter. Begin with 'Dear' and finish with 'Yours'. (Don't bother to include your address at the top right!)

If they reply in a more relaxed manner, then you can follow suit if you wish.

An email can say a lot about you – just as a letter can.

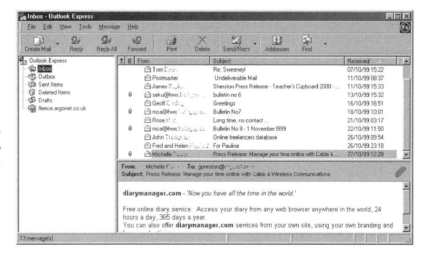

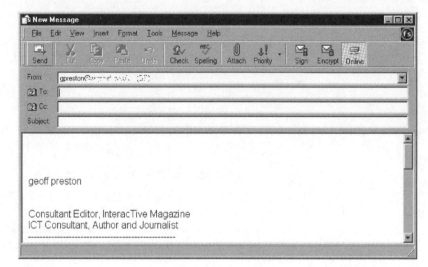

If your email program cannot automatically append a signature, try creating a signature as a text document and pasting the contents into your mailings.

Signature

Many email programs allow you to automatically append your own signature, comprising anything from your name to contact telephone numbers and even cute philosophical messages. But care should be taken not to overdo this feature. For some people, email is a serious means of communication and half a page of gibberish about your views on the meaning of life together with an extended list of ways you can be contacted may not be deemed very time-friendly. It's also not always appropriate to inflict your own musings on others.

A further development on this theme is to build up a sort of picture using keyboard characters, and include that as part of your signature. Usually the backward and forward slash ('/' and '\'), the 'greater than' and 'less than' signs ('<' and '>') and an assortment of other characters like 'O' and 'o' make up these works of art.

They can, of course, say a great deal about the sender. Personally, when I receive an email with one of these at the foot, I usually think, 'This person is paid too much for doing too little' or 'What a twit!'.

Sending an email

1 Open your email program and choose the New Message icon:

(Outlook Express)   (Netscape Messenger)

2 This will open a window into which you compose your message.

3 Enter the email address of the recipient.

The upper window is from Outlook Express, the lower from Netscape Messenger.

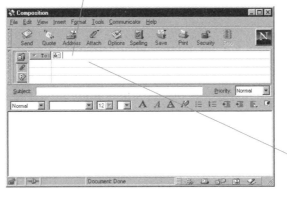

4 Enter the addresses of any copies to be sent.

5 Click in the Subject panel and type in a brief phrase for the subject.

6 Click in the main window and type your message.

7 When your message in complete, click the icon to place the message in the Out tray.

(Outlook Express)

(Netscape Messenger)

If you are currently connected to the Internet, your message can be sent immediately, but will not be sent until Send/Receive is clicked. If you're not currently connected, your message will remain in the Outbox until you next log on or click the Send/Receive button.

Replying to emails

The most popular way of replying to an email is to simply return the received mailing with your own notes added. If one applies that approach to traditionally written letters, it would be considered inappropriate, to say the very least. Yet, email programs actually encourage this approach by offering the user the opportunity of automatically including the original text when replying.

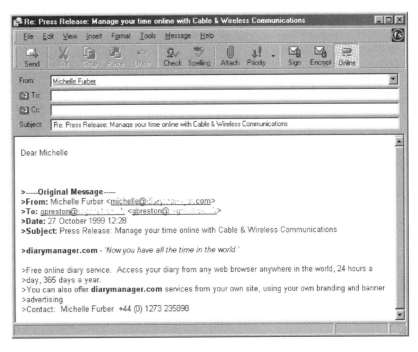

Some recipients don't like having their email returned with just a 5-word response tagged onto the bottom.

When an email arrives which requires a response, choose Reply and a new email will be generated with the recipient's name and email address included. The text from the original message will also be included but each line will be prefixed with a mark (usually '>') to denote that it has been copied from the original message. Your reply can be placed before or after the message to which you are replying, or better still, intermingled with it. For example, if the sender has made several points that each need to be addressed as a separate issue, then it's best to put your response with each point.

Forwarding an email

Received emails can easily be 'bounced' to someone else – a practice which is becoming more popular. But do beware. Sometimes emails arrive which are for you and you alone and not for sharing with the world at large. Remember, if you send an email to someone else, they can send it to another person who in turn could send it to someone else.

If you don't want an email forwarded, put a notice at the bottom to the effect that this is a private message and is not to be forwarded.

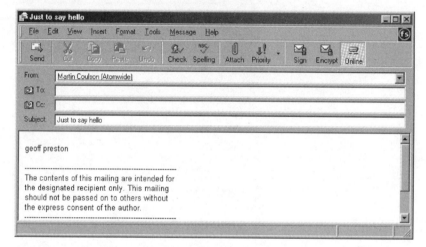

There are some occasions when an email is sent with the specific intention of passing it on to as many people as possible – virus warnings for example. If you receive a notification of a possible virus, forward it to everyone on your mailing list, even if you think it might be a hoax.

Returned email

If you incorrectly address the envelope of a traditional letter, it's unlikely to get to its intended destination. With email it's more certain – it definitely won't get there. It will simply be returned to you as undeliverable. You'll probably get a computer-generated message from a postmaster somewhere telling you it was undeliverable. The original text will usually be included with the message. Check the address and re-send.

Who has an email address?

The actual number of people who own an email address is estimated to be about 20,000,000 worldwide. The number of people who use email regularly is more difficult to establish. But the reality is that everyone probably knows someone who has an email address. You can find email addresses from the Internet by going to a site that maintains an email address database. Typical are *www.whowhere.lycos.com/* and *www.hotbot.com/*

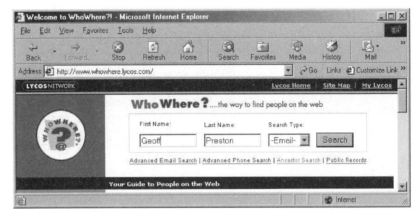

Whilst you're on this site, why don't you enter your own email address so others can find you?

Once you've arrived at the site, enter the first name and surname of the person you're trying to contact. You'll probably get several people with the same or similar names, but you should be able to locate the right one.

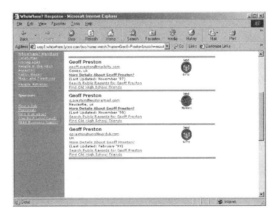

Clicking on the email address will create a new email document addressed to the correct person.

Sending documents

Don't try sending very large documents. It's really annoying when you try to collect your email and find it takes an age because someone has sent you a 5 Mb file.

In days gone by, sending files along with your emails was a long and involved process. Now, with more modern software, attaching documents is simply a case of dragging and dropping. The necessary encrypting and decoding is all done automatically in the background.

Pictures, word-processed documents and spreadsheets can all be sent as an email attachment. The recipient receives the document which can be opened immediately or saved.

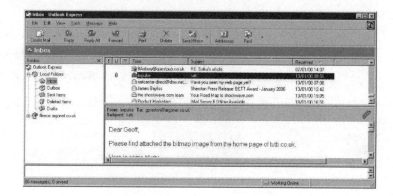

When an email is received which contains an attached file, the first thing you'll notice is that the download time is increased. Different email programs show attachments in different ways. (Outlook Express displays a paper clip symbol.)

Attachments are notorious for containing viruses – especially if the attachment was created in MS Word or Excel which can store viruses in macros.

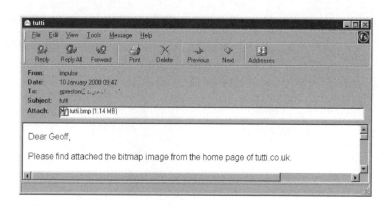

Opening the mail or clicking on the symbol reveals the attachment. Double-click on it to open it or save it to disc.

Compressing and decompressing.

If you want to send an attached file with your email, it's often best to archive (or compress) it first, especially if it contains pictures.

One of the most popular compression programs for PCs is WinZip which can be downloaded from  *www.winzip.com/.* For Mac users, try StuffIt which is available from *www.stuffit.com/*

The recipient needs to have the same program to decompress the attachment.

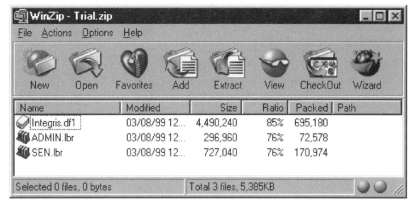

Many email systems automatically place a limit on the size of the mailing. Hotmail, for example, has a 2 Mb ceiling on emails.
 Anything above this size will be rejected.

WinZip and StuffIt will compress files and folders very efficiently so they occupy a lot less space and consequently can be sent considerably faster. But you should still watch the size of the file you are sending.

When you receive attachments they may be compressed in which case you'll usually need WinZip or StuffIt to decompress them before they can be read.

Sometimes people send a self-extracting file which simply means that, when you've downloaded it and saved it onto your local hard disc, double-clicking on the file will cause it to decompress itself without the need for a program like WinZip.

Beware when receiving attachments. Make sure you have a good virus protection program running before you attempt to open them. Even so, treat unsolicited mailings with attachments, especially from unknown sources, with extreme suspicion.

Secure delivery

Unlike handwritten and hand-signed letters, it is difficult to prove that an email came from a particular individual. Emails are now frequently used to send confidential material, where letters in sealed envelopes were previously used.

Digital IDs ensure that emailed documents are not forged and that the person who reads it is the intended recipient and nobody else. It is the equivalent of sending a letter in a sealed envelope and requiring the recipient to sign for it on delivery. You can even encrypt the message using a digital ID.

A digital ID comprises:

* a public key

* a private key

* a digital signature

To digitally sign an email, you add your digital signature and a public key to the message. This is known as a certificate.

Getting a Digital ID

1 In Outlook Express, go to Tools and select Accounts.

2 Choose the account in which you wish to have a Digital ID and click Properties.

3 Click on the Security tab

4 Choose Get Digital ID.

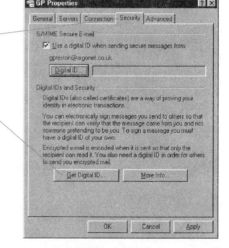

This will open a website which will allow you to choose Verisign – one of the largest providers of Digital IDs.

For a small annual fee they will provide everything required for a Digital ID, including details about setting it up and using it.

If you intend sending confidential material, always use a digital signature.

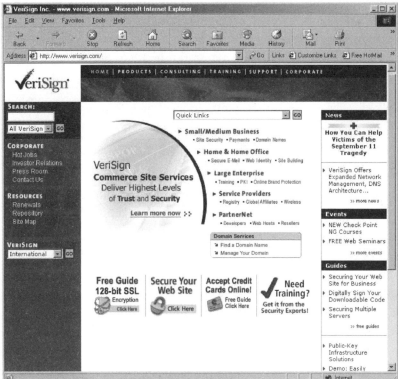

The Verisign website is at *www.verisign.com/*

Better emails

Well, not better, but different. Emails tend to look very plain and bland – rather like a telegram. Just as people send less than formal letters on fancy paper, so too can you send your social emails with a designer backdrop.

Some of the styles might not be your first choice for, say, a job application.

Rather than simply clicking on the New Message button in Outlook Express, click on Messages on the menu bar and choose New Message Using. This opens a sub-menu which allows you to choose different stationery for your email.

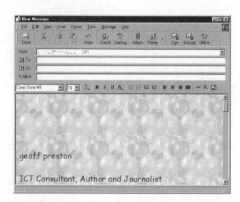

The various styles include different backgrounds, different font styles and sometimes different font colours. Quite a change from the usual black on white.

Greetings

There are dozens of sites that offer this free service, amongst them is ICQ at: *www.icq.com/greetings/* Most require the same sequence to be carried out, although there are some variations between the different sites.

This is a great way to brighten up a loved one's day.

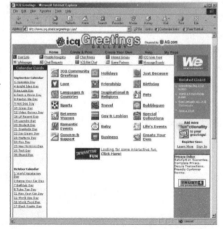

Choose a card from the hundreds available, add a greeting, enter the recipient's email address (and yours) and send it.

Recipients receive a computer generated email telling them where to collect their greeting.

Abusing the system

Just as the Internet is used for doubtful purposes, so too is email. And it's virtually impossible to bring the culprits to book because free mail services like Hotmail are anonymous and therefore virtually untraceable.

Incoming mail

In schools, this can be a serious problem. All students at a particular school will have similar email addresses. Once you know the common part it's fairly easy to get to the rest so individual students can easily be contacted. Stories abound about drug deals cooked up via school-based email services.

It's very difficult to track down the authors of inappropriate emails.

It's difficult to police because the contents of mailboxes can't always easily be accessed by others (including the network manager and the postmaster). Even if they could be accessed, trawling through hundreds, if not thousands of mailings looking for suspicious contents is not a practical proposition, even if the messages have been saved on the system.

Outgoing mail

The other problem is with inappropriate messages leaving your email account or email domain. If others use your email account or domain, there is a danger of them using the system for all manner of purposes that you may not like. Again, this is difficult to police, especially in an institution with hundreds of users.

Some email programs allow the system supervisor to create a short warning message which will be automatically tagged onto every mailing. If users know that a warning along the lines of, '*If you are offended by the contents of this mailing, please return it to...*' is automatically sent out with every email, they will usually refrain from sending anything likely to cause offence.

But, to put it into perspective, if a person wishes to send inappropriate material, they can do it with traditional letters. Email just means they don't have to walk to the postbox.

Email annoyances

A whole new culture has developed around the use of email. This development has accelerated noticeably during the last three or four years when computers have become much more widely available and are now being sold with Internet connectivity built-in.

Built-in Internet connectivity means, by definition, built-in email as part of the computer package on sale in the same shop that sells washing machines and hi-fi. When you buy a washing machine, you get a manual telling you how to wash clothes. When you buy a computer you don't get a manual telling you how to use email.

Regrettably many people find themselves with email included in their new computer package but don't really know how to handle it properly. For them it's a hobby. For others it is more serious.

In the order of my own personal annoyance:

If you don't want an email forwarded, put a notice at the bottom to the effect that this is a private message and is not to be forwarded.

1. There is a growing assumption that emails should be replied to immediately, or at least within the hour. Some people seem to think that your life involves little more than sitting in front of the computer waiting for emails to roll in. If you don't respond immediately they send another complaining that you haven't responded to the first. The very nature of email encourages this desire for immediate action and reaction. Previously, a letter would be handwritten and taken to the postbox. A reminder would not have been sent until (usually) at least a week had passed. Be patient, do not expect an instant reply, even though emails are delivered more or less instantly.

    However, that said, it's worth having a standard reply message that you can quickly send which basically says you've received an email and you will respond to it in due course.

2. Recipients seem to think it's acceptable to distribute your mail to whoever they see fit. This should not be done unless you are specifically invited to do so. A friend of mine sent an email to a group of people and one of them decided to publish it in a local parish magazine without even asking him. (And without even attempting to correct some of the

mistakes which are almost inevitable if you're composing an email on a palmtop computer in the middle of Tanzania.)

This practice is not on. After all, you wouldn't consider photocopying a letter you received and distributing it to anyone and everyone.

3. People seem to have trouble knowing how to construct an email. If writing a letter using pen and paper, the normal salutation is *Dear Sir, Dear Jill*, or *Dear Revd Barber*. Emails seem to discourage this approach and as a result you get greetings like *Hi Pete, Hello*, or no salutation whatsoever. If it's a formal email, be on the safe side and begin *Dear...* If replying to an email, it's probably safest to use the same format as was sent. Although I do draw the line at copying salutations such as *Hi-ya Geoff, Watchya Mate* and *Howsitgoin' Sport*.

TLAs

AKA (also known as) three-letter acronyms, these result from either laziness or just simply 2M2D (too much to do). They have been used in emails FSY (for several years) and are analogous to, and about as understandable to outsiders as CRS (Cockney Rhyming Slang).

Too many TLAs makes text DTR (difficult to read).

Rather than writing out the whole phrase, it is reduced to its SPA (smallest possible abbreviation) which is a group of (usually) three letters, which ideally SFAW (should form a word) and PSV (preferably something vulgar). WAL (with any luck) the recipient will understand WYM (what you mean) but often they just leave the reader LOL (laughing out loud).

OWOW (one word of warning); some of these TLAs are TUB (totally and utterly bogus)!

Smileys

Emails can seem a little aggressive if they're put together too quickly.

To try and lighten them, or to try to ensure the recipient reads the message in the same tone as it was written, some people include 'smiley faces' (sometimes referred to as emoticons) in their messages.

Personally I'd rather receive an email that was written in such a way that the underlying tone could not be misunderstood. (I don't remember ever reading a paper-based letter punctuated with smiley faces.)

Some of the most common are (and these are usually read sideways):

:-)	I'm happy/pleased
:-D	I'm laughing
:-(	I'm sad/angry/cross
:-|	I have no particular emotion
;-)	I have a raised eyebrow
:-O	I am shocked
:'-(	I am crying
:-*	I am kissing you
:-P	I am sticking out my tongue
:-)>	I've got a beard (actually, I haven't)
8-)	I'm wearing glasses (actually, I'm not)
:-X	I won't say a word

Reading too many of these may make you want to go for a pint of (_)] (not read sideways).

If you feel you need to use one of these, try re-wording your message so you don't need to.

Newsgroups

This chapter introduces newsgroups and outlines what they are and how you can access them. It goes on to explain how to post your own articles and how to stay out of trouble with the other members of the group.

Covers

Chapter Six

What is a newsgroup?

Many people have tried to explain what a newsgroup is by weaving a witty analogy which invariably gives away the author's feelings on the subject. The truth is that these homespun philosophical gems are, in the main, correct although I've yet to find one that fully explains a newsgroup.

So as not to disappoint, try this:

One definition

A newsgroup is rather like a large receptacle into which you can place any number of pieces of paper containing questions, an answer to a question, personal feelings, whatever you like.

At any time you can dive into the receptacle, read any of the pieces of paper and if you wish, reply to some of them.

If you wish to quote this analogy, replace each occurrence of 'receptacle' with 'filing cabinet' if you approve of newsgroups, or 'dustbin' if you don't.

The only restriction is that the contents of each receptacle should be on the same subject. The receptacle is clearly labelled with the name of the subject and although there is nothing to stop you putting in a piece of paper with a question about another totally unrelated subject, there wouldn't be much point because it will probably be discarded.

(If you go to the receptacle expecting to find comments about subject X and you pull out a piece of paper relating to subject Y, you too would probably discard it.)

As the author of a piece of paper that you placed in the wrong receptacle, you might even get a lecture about what the receptacle is for and where you should have placed your piece of paper.

Certain individuals have seen newsgroups as a route to cheap (i.e. free) advertising.

They go around dumping adverts into the receptacles, usually when you're looking through them, so that they land, not amongst all the other pieces of paper, but on the top so that they're right under your nose.

One more thing: my ISP alone hosts over 32,000 receptacles. Each receptacle can (and frequently does) hold thousands of pieces of paper from all round the world.

Whoever coined the phrase 'information overload' was certainly familiar with newsgroups.

Newsgroups have been referred to as the Internet equivalent of Speaker's Corner in Hyde Park, London where anyone can go and stand on a soap box and pontificate. Newsgroups have also been described as electronic whingeing, hi-tech gossip and computerised scare-mongering.

More positively, they have been described as electronic billboards where people can post articles and others can reply to them.

Newsgroup addressing

The name of a newsgroup provides the description of the subject.

In general terms, the name takes the form:

<type>.<category>.<topic>

For example:

rec.video.production

The type is recreational and the category is video. The topic within that the video category is production.

Some of the most common newsgroup types are:

This list doesn't even represent the 'tip of the iceberg'.

alt.	Alternative
bionet.	Biological
biz.	Business
comp.	Computer
microsoft.	Support for MS software
misc.	Miscellaneous discussions
news.	Usenet discussions
rec.	Recreational activities
sci.	Scientific discussions
soc.	Social and religious discussion
talk.	Anything controversial

Newsgroup types that begin with the name of a country (fr, de, be, es, uk etc.) are subjects of particular interest to nationals of that country and will often be in the language of that country.

What do you need?

If you have Outlook Express or Netscape Messenger then you have everything you need to access newsgroups.

Specifying a News Server

You'll first need to enter the name of your News Server into Outlook Express or Netscape Messenger.

(Outlook Express)

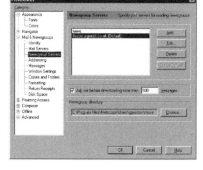

(Netscape Messenger)

Your Internet installation disc may have done this for you.

In Outlook Express go to Tools on the menu bar, open Accounts and click on the News tab. For Netscape Messenger, go to Edit on the menu bar, choose Preferences and click on Newsgroup servers.

You'll then have to enter the name of the News Server which will be provided by your Internet Service Provider.

Typically, the name of the News Server will be along the lines of:

<name>.<isp name>.com

Stick to one server – the one provided by your ISP.

You can use as many News Servers as you wish, but there's not usually a great deal of point as many of the newsgroups will be duplicated, and even if that were not the case, one News Server will provide far more information than one person can possibly cope with. Servers such as Pipex host most of the newsgroups and the only ones they don't host are the 'undesirable' ones.

Downloading the newsgroup list

This can take a considerable amount of time – up to 60 minutes depending on speed of connection and the number of groups hosted by your ISP. Fortunately, this only has to be done once.

(Outlook Express)

(Netscape Messenger)

The number of newsgroups is staggering. My server hosts over 32,000 but there are probably twice that number worldwide. Some are not very popular, but others (like the newsgroups dedicated to the finer points of Microsoft's Windows) have a huge number of readers.

Registering

When all of the newsgroup names have been downloaded, you can decide which groups you wish to use (or subscribe to). You can add to the list and remove groups from your list as often as you like, but initially you should restrict yourself to just one or two groups which specialise in a subject in which you have at least some knowledge, if not expertise.

Subscribing to (joining) newsgroups is free.

Initially register for 1 or 2 groups only. You can always add more later.

To subscribe to a newsgroup, (using either Outlook Express or Netscape Messenger) select the group and click on the Subscribe button. To unsubscribe, click on the Unsubscribe button. A flag will appear at the left showing which groups you are subscribed to. Clicking the button labelled Subscribed or Subscribed Groups will list only those groups you are subscribed to.

Searching for a newsgroup

To make life a little easier, both news readers provide a search facility so that you can quickly find newsgroups within a particular topic. If you enter a name in the search panel, you're sure to find something.

Always use a search rather than trying to wade through the list by hand.

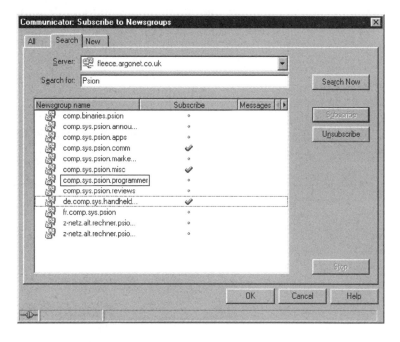

Even topics that one might think are fairly small and specialised can contain several newsgroups, when one might think there wasn't even enough interest to sustain one group.

A search for *Psion* (the manufacturers of hand-held computers/ organisers) for example, reveals 12 newsgroups. Select the one(s) you wish to subscribe to and they will be added to your list of subscribed groups.

When you're more familiar with newsgroups, try entering 'magic' or 'music' to get some information about other topics.

Even when you're more familiar with newsgroups, it's unlikely you'll need to subscribe to more than half-a-dozen. Even with half that number, the amount of articles that will be generated will be enormous.

Downloading the news

All of the messages in your registered newsgroups can now be downloaded.

There are two ways of going about this. You can either download the headers only (that is, the titles of each of the articles) or you can download the headers together with the articles themselves.

Downloading the headers only takes a very short time, but to read the articles you'll have to go online. If you download the headers and the documents together, it will take considerably longer, but you can then read the documents offline.

Unless there are very few documents, download only the headers first.

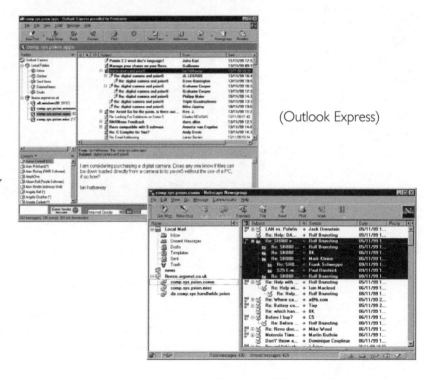

(Outlook Express)

(Netscape Messenger)

The documents are grouped together so that you have the initial document, with the various responses to it. This means that you can follow the discussion even if you joined halfway through it.

Reading an article

If the actual article has not been downloaded with the header then you will need to go online to read it.

With the news reader open so that the headers are listed, you can read any of the articles by simply clicking on one of them to show the text in the panel below the list of headers.

The articles will be grouped so that the original article is on top, and the responses made by others will be immediately underneath. If you see a plus sign alongside a header, clicking on it will show all of the responses relating to the original article. (This can be clearly seen in the screenshots of both Outlook Express and Netscape Messenger on the facing page).

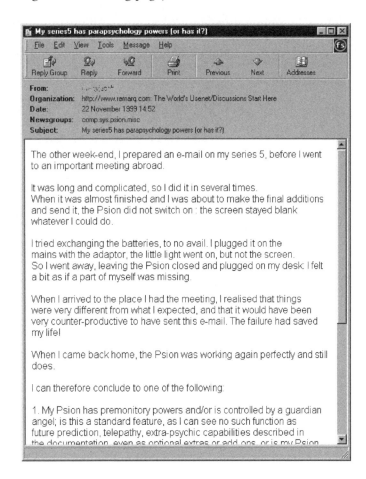

Articles can be about anything from simple questions to bizarre anecdotal jottings.

Alternatively, double-clicking on the header will open the article in a window of its own. You must do this if you wish to print an article.

Responding to an article

After spending some time browsing through the articles and messages that have been placed on the newsgroups, you will almost certainly be drawn in to replying to some. Even if it's only to answer a question to get someone out of a fix.

You can respond either to the group (in which case your response will be added to the list of responses) or you can respond to the originator personally, which is effectively sending an email.

It's more personal if you reply by email.

The Reply Group (Outlook Express) or Reply All (Netscape Messenger) buttons will send your reply to the group. The Reply button will send your reply to the author only.

Either way, type in your reply as you would for an email and click the Send button.

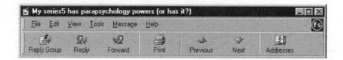

The Reply buttons will send an email reply to the author of the currently displayed message which need not be the author of the original article – in other words, you can reply to one of the replies.

Synchronising

If you can, choose to download only the changes.

New postings to newsgroups arrive very quickly and you'll be able to see your replies almost as soon as you've posted them. You must, however, first refresh the newsgroup's content by clicking on the Synchronise button. This will match all of the headers on your computer with the headers on the server. You should then be able to see your replies (assuming you can find the original article again).

Posting an article

It won't be long before you've been bitten by the bug and want to make your own views known, or feel that this is a suitable forum to try to get answers to some of those burning questions you've been wanting to pose for most of your adult life.

To post an article, select the newsgroup you wish to use and click on the New Post button.

Respond to articles before attempting to post your own. This will give you a better idea of the sort of topics covered by the group.

A window will open looking exactly the same as if it were an email and even carrying your signature (if you set one up for your email).

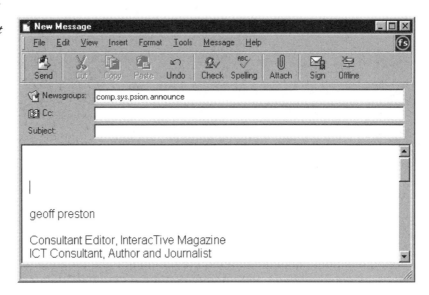

Just as with email, enter your message and send it using the Send button.

Attachments

Avoid downloading Word documents at all costs – they can contain some hateful viruses hidden within macros.

In addition to the textual part of your article, you can also send files including pictures and fully formatted word-processed documents.

Great care should be taken when opening attachments to newsgroup postings as they can contain viruses. In general, only include attachments in the binary (bin.) newsgroups.

Netiquette

Newsgroups have no formal rules, although many have a sort of 'code of conduct' which you are expected to adhere to. The 'rules' can usually be found in FAQ – Frequently Asked Questions. This is known as Netiquette.

The first thing is to ensure you are posting to the correct group – you'll receive a lot of flak if you don't.

Flame wars

Never get involved in a slanging match, known as a flame war. All you'll do is lower yourself to the level of the other person. The trouble is (and this comment will generate a lot of response on the newsgroups) that once someone has sent an email, typed a letter and got to level 2 of the latest video game, they think they're an expert in the field of computing in general (and the Internet in particular) and could have a one-to-one discussion with Bill Gates. You'll never win against people like that, so don't try.

Some newsgroups and newsgroup users have been around for a long time. It's familiar territory for them, but not necessarily for the newcomer.

Don't shout

Capital letters means you're shouting. If you send a message with Caps Lock on, people will think you're being aggressive.

Advertising

Don't post commercial messages in newsgroups. This is called 'spam' and it's not very popular. If you want to advertise, try the business (biz.) groups which were set up for that reason. (The trouble is that nobody ever reads them because they're full of adverts.) But even so, don't post them anywhere else.

If you stick within those boundaries, you're unlikely to fall foul of anyone.

Interaction

This chapter shows you how to communicate with people from around the world using your keyboard to 'talk' and your mouse to 'move'. You can even play board games and card games. Unlike email, this interaction is in real time.

Covers

Chapter Seven

What are Chatlines?

Adults should be aware that, like telephone chatlines, these are a constant source of fascination for teenagers.

Although on the face of it, Internet chat seems like a trivial feature, it has its serious uses and has been put to serious use on more than a few occasions.

Since its introduction in the late 1980s, news reporters have used it to transmit accounts of a diverse range of events from the World Cup to the Gulf War.

The reality is that Internet chat is most frequently used as a harmless means of social gossip. A group of people from different cultures and on different sides of the world can communicate with each other in real-time without running up a huge phone bill.

The darker side of this topic is that it can be host to some conversations which at best can only be described as undesirable, punctuated with language which is best described as repetitive.

For the home or school user, chat programs do offer the opportunity to communicate with others from other cultures and have been successfully used to support the teaching of some foreign languages.

There are three main chat techniques available to the user:

If you want to join in, you'll need to be fairly proficient on the keyboard.

*   Webchat

*   Internet Relay Chat

*   Instant messaging

To the casual onlooker, it's actually quite difficult to tell the first two apart. The output is rows of text preceded by the name (or nickname) of the person who wrote it.

The message here is that online chat should be monitored even more closely than Internet use in general. It's a message that I make no apology for repeating.

Webchat

About the easiest way to get started with chatter is to go to Yahoo's chatrooms.

As with all of Yahoo's services, you'll need to register by going to their home page at *www.yahoo.com/* (signing up with Yahoo also gives you free access to other Yahoo services). Each time you visit the chat site, you'll have to 'sign-on' by entering your Yahoo ID and your password.

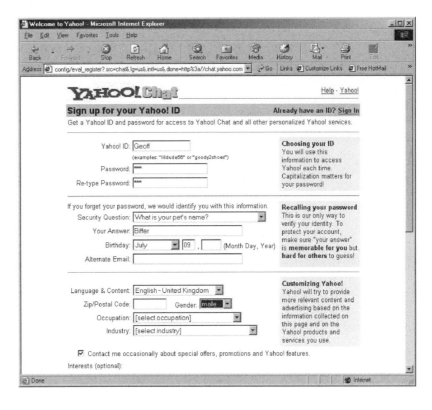

You'll have to register on most of the chat systems. Try to use the same name and password, or keep a note of them all in a text file or database.

Once you've registered, you can start chatting immediately, although you will receive confirmation by email within 24 hours.

Like so many chatlines, Yahoo's is divided into areas called 'rooms'. Entering a chatroom is rather like entering a real room – it may be empty or full, or there may be just a few people present.

Each chatroom is given a name which reflects the topic of conversation you can expect to take part in within that room.

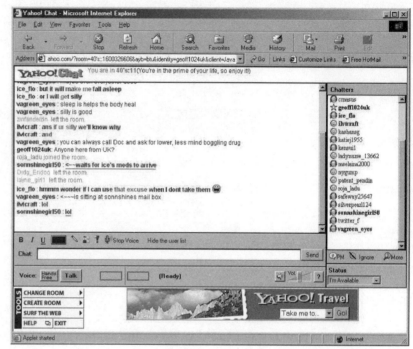

This is a great way to improve your typing skills.

You're unlikely to have a deep and meaningful conversation with an intellectual academic.

You can change chatrooms at any time by clicking the CHANGE ROOM icon at the bottom left of the screen. In the centre panel will be a list of subjects to choose. When you've selected a subject, on the right will be a list of specific topics within that subject. Alongside each topic will be a number telling you how many people are currently in the room. You'll need to find a room that's got more than 1 person, but not dozens or, in some cases, hundreds.

Clicking on the subject will take you into the room where you will be announced as:

<name> has just entered <room>.

The panel just above Tools (labelled Chat:) is your 'mouth'. Type into the panel and press Return to be heard.

Some people take the trouble to colour or embolden their text so that it stands out from the rest.

Unlike a conventional room, the conversation can be 'heard' by everyone in the room although you can, if you wish, have a private conversation with one of the group. On the right of the screen will be a list of visitors to the room and right-clicking one of the names enables you to find out more about that person and to have a private chat with them.

If children are using this feature, it needs to be very carefully monitored.

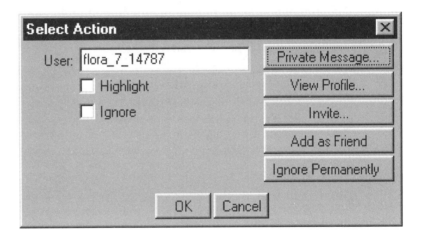

Yahoo chat will also give you access to the so-called Adult rooms. These areas are entered via a warning sign pointing out that you should be 18 to enter. For those who are over 18, enter only if you are not offended. For those over 18 who have children under 18, monitor the use of this chat facility very carefully. This chatline is available to all, it's very easy to register and very easy to access.

Look out also for advertised events in Yahoo's chat rooms. Occasionally they have special guests available who you can talk to. Celebrities have included a stress consultant, a dermatologist and a wine expert.

For information about the best webchat rooms, go to:

www.user.globalnet.co.uk/~peter18/chatrooms.html

Internet Relay Chat

Internet Relay Chat is rather like the Internet equivalent of CB radio with its own language and customs. It was developed in the late 1980s by Jarkko Oikarinen, a Finnish programmer, and has proved enormously popular.

To use IRC you need to download a small program. If you're using a PC with Windows you need to go to *www.mirc.co.uk/*, whilst Apple Macintosh users should go to *www.ircle.com/*

The software arrives as a self-extracting file and running it will extract the parts and install it. (These modules are usually shareware which means you get it free for a month after which you have to pay a small fee to keep it going.)

There is a list of commands that really need to be understood before embarking on IRC.

Getting Started

When the software has been installed, run it and the About mIRC window will be displayed which will enable you to register and visit the website should you wish to do so.

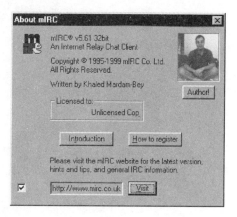

If you're not connected to the Internet, the program will dial your default connection.

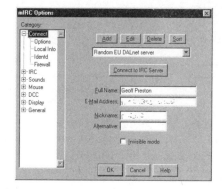

Close the About mIRC window and the mIRC Options window will open which contains your registration details. The only information you need to put here each time is the name you wish to be known by in this session. When you click on the Connect to IRC Server button, you should get online, but if not, try changing the server by selecting another from the list above the Connect to IRC Server button.

You don't use your browser for IRC – it's all done through the downloaded software.

The next window to appear gives you the chance to choose which channel (or room, as it is generally known) to use. At any time during your IRC session you can leave one room and visit another. The rooms are supposed to be named in such a way that the user has at least a clue as to what the topics of conversation are likely be. Unfortunately this is not always the case and finding a suitable place is often a matter of trial and error.

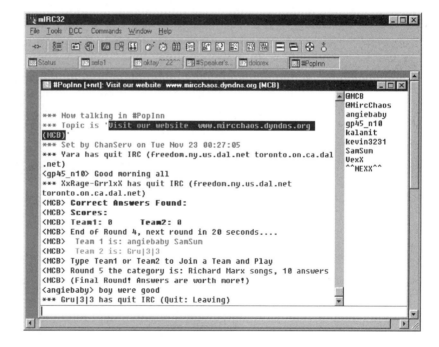

Some people get together and form teams and have a sort of quiz. Right-clicking on one of the names on the right means that you can confer with other team members without the opposition knowing what you're saying.

Instant messaging

Both webchat and IRC are public meeting places that you drop into in the hope that you'll find somebody worth talking to. But even if you do get a good conversation going, others tend to interrupt.

This has led to the development of Instant Messaging or 'buddies' as it is sometimes referred to. All the big players have their own version of it (AOL's Instant Messenger, Microsoft's Messenger, etc.) but top of the pile is ICQ (I seek you).

You need to download the program from *www.icq .com/* which is available free for a trial period, after which there is a small fee for the licence.

The idea is that you set up a list of contacts (buddies) and when you and they are online, you can 'talk' to each other in private.

This is live, real-time conversation.

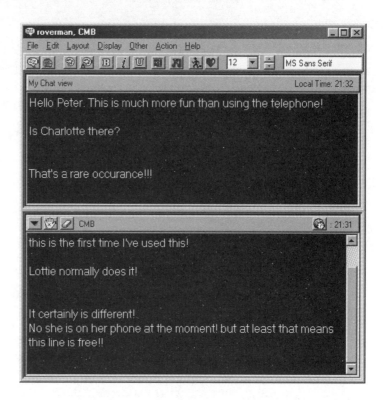

When it's running, you have a window with two areas – one that you type into, and one to display the text your buddy enters.

Once ICQ has been downloaded and installed, you'll need to register after which you will be given an ID number. You'll also need to choose a name which you will be known by. ICQ loads automatically when you switch your computer on and it sits on the Taskbar at the bottom right of the screen. It doesn't do much until you go online when it 'announces' itself to the world at large.

This is a good way of communicating with people overseas without running up a huge telephone bill.

When it's active, the icon changes to a flower, which can also be seen in the ICQ menu, displayed by clicking the icon on the Taskbar.

From time to time, if you're online, you'll get a request to have a chat. The request will pop-up on the screen and contain details of the person requesting the chat. If you agree, the dialogue window will open and you can now chat.

ICQ will announce when one of your buddies comes online, so you'll be able to decide whether to have a chat. Similarly, when you go online, you'll be told which of your buddies is also online.

This can be distracting if you're online as it gives people the opportunity to disrupt you for a chat.

If you get tired of random people trying to strike up a meeting, you can put ICQ into dormant mode which means it's still running, but nobody can see you, although you can still see them.

If you're bored, you can try to set up a chat with someone else. This could be a random chat, or a chat with one of your buddies.

Again, this is real-time chat, but the real fascination is watching the other person typing. The letters come up one at a time as they are being typed. You can even see when they've made a spelling mistake and are trying to correct it.

Interactive games

This is an interesting variation on the theme of chatting.

The web provides a meeting place for all sorts. If you enjoy playing games, then you can play against others who you will never have seen before, and who possibly hail from the other side of the world.

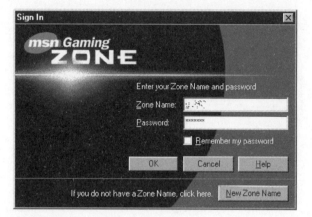

The Gaming Zone is one of the most popular sites for people to chat and play a game at the same time. The site features mainly board games and card games which you play online with others.

When you first visit the site you must register by providing the obligatory username and password. The popularity of this site is such that almost any meaningful username you enter will return a message telling you that that name has already been taken and suggesting half-a-dozen alternatives.

Initially there is a little setting up to do, but it is well worth it.

You'll next have to download some software which takes only a short while but provides you with access to the main areas of the Gaming Zone.

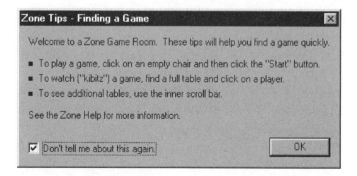

...cont'd

In future, whenever you log on to the Gaming Zone, you will have to enter your username and password.

The options default to leaving you contactable all the time you're online.

A window will be displayed showing that you are logged on and providing you with some menus which will display your current status.

You choose a particular game from the list on the first page of the website and when you've made your choice you'll be taken to that particular zone where there are a number of rooms in which people will be playing the game you selected.

Respect the room levels. If you are a novice, don't go into the room where there are competitions in progress.

When you play a particular type of game for the first time you'll have to download a small module. After that, you will be free to visit any of the rooms in that zone.

Conveniently, each room carries a sign telling the visitor of the likely standard of play within.

The Gaming Zone is at: *www.zone.com/*

Virtual reality

Cybertown is a virtual reality city which you can become part of and in which you can interact with others.

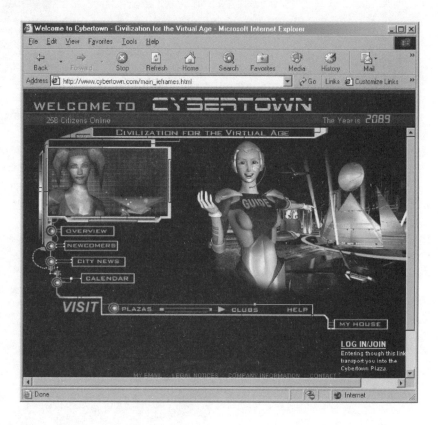

You enter Cybertown at *www.cybertown.com/* and although you can take a limited part in the proceedings, to really get involved you need to register.

The email arrives virtually immediately.

This involves entering a username and a password. There are several thousand people here so you'll need to choose something that hasn't already been taken. You must also enter your email address and you will then be issued with an immigration code (password) to allow you into Cybertown.

Once you've registered and logged on you will be given an 'avatar'. This is 'you' in the virtual world and you move your avatar around Cybertown and interact with others.

Cybertown is a 3D world which you become part of, and where you live out your virtual life with others who come and go. Just like real life.

If you know a friend who visits Cybertown, entering their username will get them some bonus points when you register.

Living in Cybertown is not simply a case of roaming around chatting to people you happen to bump into; you really do need to get involved. You'll need, for example to get a job and find somewhere to live. Having said that, you can chat to others; indeed, you need to help each other to a large extent.

This is a game and there is a points scoring system which you need to be aware of. If you can't find anyone to help you, there is a help page which shows you how to buy food, get a job and generally live your virtual life to the full.

MUDs

Multi User Dungeons (MUDs) have been around for several years but modern high-speed computing has meant that whereas MUDs once looked rather like the output from a chatline, they now have superb graphics. This is an adventure game played by lots of people from around the world and lavishly illustrated:

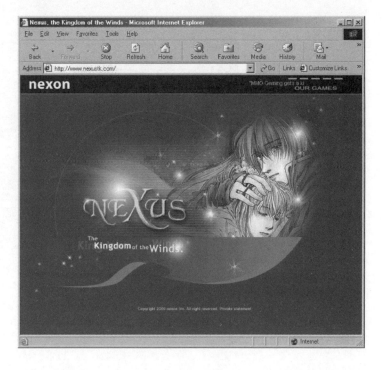

This is addictive.

Nexon is one of several sites which offers users the chance to visit different locations, interact with the others and, specifically, to achieve a goal.

You choose an identity (which comes with an avatar) and you are given the opportunity to speak by entering text, and to issue commands by typing special codes.

If you do decide to try one of these sites, you'll need a fast computer (and connection) as you're downloading some very large graphics.

To join in, you'll usually need to download a module which is available from the site. Nexus is at: *www.nexustk.com/*

Bargains for all?

This chapter shows how the Internet can be used to buy goods and services from the comfort of your own armchair.

Covers

Chapter Eight

The ultimate retail therapy?

Mail order shopping is almost as old as the concept of shopping itself. For years we have posted orders for a huge range of goods which have been advertised in catalogues, magazines or even the morning newspaper. Anything from nails to underwear, from saucepans to armchairs have at some stage been offered by mail order.

In most cases an order form was printed with the advertisement and, when completed by the bargain-hungry customer, was placed in an envelope together with payment (usually a cheque) and sent to the supplier who in return dispatched the goods.

Newspapers still carry lots of mail order adverts.

The stock phrase of the day, *"Please allow 21 days for delivery"*, was because the time taken for the order to arrive by post, for the supplier to process it, package the merchandise and send it off by parcel post, was often that long. Or even longer if demand outstripped supply. Remember, in some cases these orders arrived at the supplier in their thousands. No wonder perishable foods didn't figure very highly in the mail order market.

The advent of credit cards has, to a very large extent, contributed to the more recent popularity of telephone mail ordering. From the retailer's viewpoint, it immediately eliminated the 4 or 5 day wait for cheque clearance. For the customer, quoting a credit card number means that it is no longer necessary to send a letter, as the primary reason for the letter was to deliver payment, which the credit card replaced.

It is now unnecessary to fill out a form, write a cheque or wander off to the post box. All the customer needs to do is pick up the phone, dial a number (usually a freephone number), place the order and pay by quoting a credit card number.

You don't even need to leave your armchair – let alone your house.

And now, you don't need to read either because there are countless shopping channels on television, so all you need is the TV remote control in one hand and the phone in the other. Armchair shopping is hugely popular but has one significant drawback – you can't go armchair shopping for a specific item. The items offered for sale are selected by the TV channel and they are offered one at a time in sequence. It's rather like sitting in front of a conveyor belt watching the goods come past and waiting until something appears that might be of use to you. You choose to either buy or not buy, and then wait for the next item to be offered for sale. You can't go TV shopping with a specific list of items.

New technology has brought together all of the best features of the other selling methods and wrapped them up in the hi-tech Internet and newly hatched e-commerce.

Most TV shopping channels operate a sort of conveyor belt system.

Shopping using the Internet opens up a whole new world of armchair shopping which is going to become far more widespread.

Numerous companies around the world have been selling via the Internet for years. Some have branched out and now offer online shopping as an alternative to their conventional retail outlets, whilst some companies have set themselves up as online only retailers. These companies don't have shops, just huge warehouses to dispatch orders.

The idea is simple. Previously, if you wanted a book, you'd go to a bookshop. Now, if you want a book, you go online to a virtual bookshop and order it from there. In the real bookshop you would pay by cash, cheque or credit card, in the virtual bookshop you can't use cash, but you can pay by credit or debit card.

Unlike television shopping, Internet shopping allows you to go to the place which sells the items you want to buy.

The weekly groceries

I can spend any amount of time browsing in music shops, computer shops and car showrooms, but top of my list of undesirable activities is food shopping. Followed closely by clothes shopping.

As with all online shopping, you don't have to be physically present in the shop to do your shopping. This means you can shop at any hour of the day or night.

If, like me, you don't enjoy trundling round a supermarket with a shopping trolley that refuses to go where you want it to, being pushed and trodden on by scores of other shoppers who are also fighting to keep their trolley in order, Internet shopping may be for you.

There are now hundreds of retailers worldwide who offer a delivery service to shoppers who, rather than visiting a store in person, choose their goods over the Internet.

Whatever is available at a Tesco store, for example, can also be purchased over the Internet and will be delivered for a small fee. Tesco introduced online shopping in 1997 and provided customers who held a Tesco loyalty card with a free CD ROM which was used to set up their computer with a sort of inventory of items.

Today, even the setup and registration can be done online by visiting *www.tesco.co.uk/* and clicking on 'Shopping', followed by 'Groceries from your local Tesco'.

Most stores, including Tesco, no longer require a loyalty card.

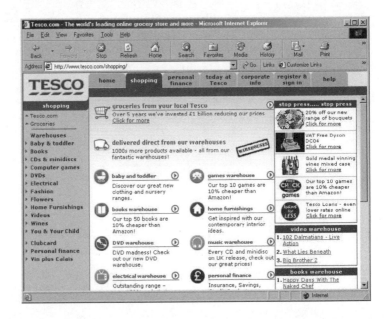

The next screen is divided into two halves: one for those already registered and one for new customers (i.e. those new to shopping at Tesco on the Internet).

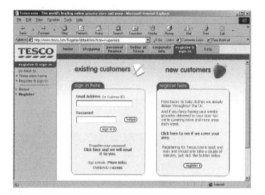

Keep your customer ID safe – you'll need it each time you shop.

If you are new, the first task is to register and for that you'll need to enter your name, address and telephone number. If you have a Tesco Club Card you should also enter the number so that you will receive the same benefits you would have if you were shopping in the store.

You will also need to choose a password which you will have to enter twice to ensure you've got it right. The system will generate a customer ID number.

Many supermarkets offer a similar service and more and more are coming online – a trend which is likely to continue. To find out more about Tesco's Home Shopping, begin by going to *www.tesco.co.uk/*.

Once you've registered, you must sign-on each time you wish to shop and this involves entering your customer ID and your password.

All the usual benefits – such as discounts that you would get by attending the shop in person, (loyalty card points, 'three-for-two' etc.) – are passed on to you as an Internet shopper.

At present, just about all Internet shops provide you with a sort of menu system through which you must 'track-down' each item you wish to buy.

To add, say, fruit juice to your basket, click on the Departments link on the left panel and the contents of the panel will change to show the different departments. About half way down will be the Soft Drinks department and in there will be a variety of drinks including fruit juices. Clicking on this link will display all the fruit juices Tesco stocks and clicking on one (or more) will place it in your basket.

At any time you can remove items from your basket and when you've been round the store and collected everything you need you can visit the checkout.

You don't have to do all your shopping in one go. You can add to your basket then return to it later to continue your shopping.

You can choose multiple items from each area. Don't forget to click the 'add to basket' button after each selection.

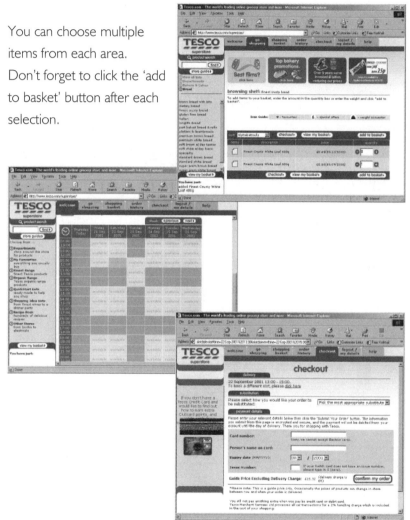

Create a file of items you use every week and begin your shopping list with these.

Delivery and Payment

When you click a Checkout button you will first be shown a timetable of available delivery times. Once you've chosen a delivery slot from the list of those available, you proceed to the checkout where you pay with a credit or debit card.

Buying software

One of the major growth areas of Internet selling is computer software. It makes a great deal of sense for both the seller and purchaser to buy over the Internet.

From the seller's point of view, there are fewer overheads. Programs are now so large that they have to be distributed either on a pile of floppy discs or CD ROM – which is now the cheaper of the two options, providing you have enough sales to warrant the cost of producing them.

Selling software over the Internet eliminates the need to hold any stock whatsoever. When someone buys a program, they merely make a copy of the file and pull it across the Internet. It means that transportation costs are now nil.

Compressed, self-extracting files can be moved very quickly over the Net.

From the buyer's point of view, you're not paying for huge quantities of fancy packaging which goes straight in the bin. That, of course, significantly reduces the cost. Quite complex programs can be packaged into a single file, which, when the end-user runs it, will self-unpack and decompress. This feature, together with faster and faster Internet access times, means that software can be downloaded very quickly.

Furthermore, the buyer doesn't need to physically go anywhere to buy the software. It can all be done from the purchaser's home.

This effectively means the end of the printed manual. What happens now is that, wrapped up in the downloaded software package, is the manual as either a text file or a HTML file (which can be viewed with a browser). Sometimes both. The end result is that the user has to either:

- juggle the new software on screen with the software manual

- print out the manual at his or her own expense, or:

- buy the relevant 'in easy steps' book

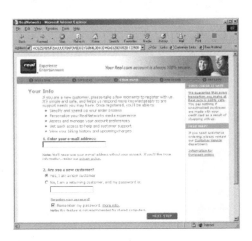

You'll almost always be asked to enter your email address. Some companies will also ask you to enter a password so that you can easily enter the site again.

As soon as you get the invoice displayed, print it for your records.

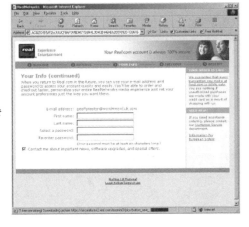

2 You'll need to enter your credit card details and also your full address – for verification purposes.

Take a note of any serial numbers or passwords given in the email.

When you've completed the appropriate sections, the company will check your details (including checking that the credit card is valid). You'll then have an invoice displayed showing what you purchased, the date and price etc.

When that is done, you'll be able to go to the download page to download your purchase.

Good companies such as this one will follow up your order with an email which will again include full details of your purchase.

Going, going, gone...

... to the lady wearing the grey coat and scratching her left ear.

Auctions can be great fun, so I'm told, but if you're frightened of finding that you've bought something because you sneezed at the wrong time, or you scratched your ear just before the gavel fell, why not try an Internet Auction?

The way it works is very clever. Once you've chosen something you want to bid for, you place a maximum bid with the auction house. Nobody else knows what you will be prepared to bid up to as the information is fed into a computer. When all the maximum bids are in, the computer effectively opens the bidding, takes bids, disregards people who have reached their limit and finally finishes up with a buyer.

There's no danger of overbidding here.

The buyer will have purchased the item by outbidding the other bidders, but will not have gone beyond his predetermined limit – one of the inherent dangers when bidding in a 'real' auction.

To try your hand at an online auction, go to *www.ebid.co.uk/*

Airline booking

Booking a flight used to be a painfully long-winded process which always seemed to require a great deal more paperwork than seemed necessary. Certainly, given the choice, I'd rather book a train journey than a plane journey (apart from the destination).

EasyJet proudly boasts that theirs is a ticketless booking system which you can book yourself over the Internet without having to go and sit in a stuffy travel agent's shop.

This is by far the easiest way to book an airline ticket.

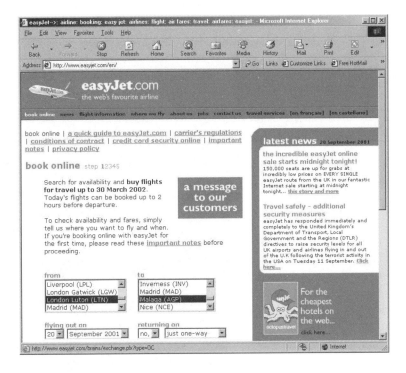

Once the booking form has been opened, you are led step by step through a series of screens into which you insert destination and departure locations and the dates on which you wish to fly.

A selection of outward and return flights will be listed and you select the ones you want before clicking the Next button. Finally you are asked to enter your credit card details for payment.

EasyJet will confirm your booking by email. The EasyJet website is *www.easyjet.co.uk/*. The site also includes online booking for car hire and car parking.

Finance – Internet banking

Most Banks and Building Societies now offer their customers banking via the Internet. The advantage is that you can make transactions, order statements and carry out a variety of other banking tasks from the comfort of your home and at any time of the day or night, 365 days a year. The only thing you can't do is actually withdraw cash – you still need to go to a 'real' bank for that.

First Direct is a branch of HSBC which began offering a very successful 24-hour telephone banking service where customers simply dial a local telephone number and get balances, move money, arrange loans and generally do most things they would do in a traditional bank.

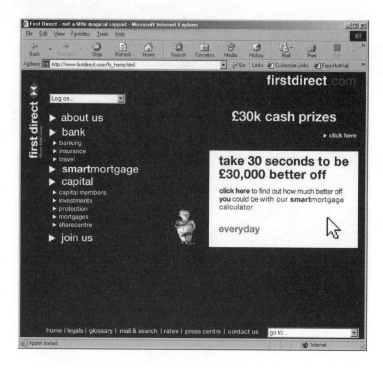

First Direct followed this success by introducing Internet banking to run alongside the telephone service and this too has become very popular. Once enrolled, you will be provided with a CD ROM containing all the software required which is installed on your PC. When the software has been installed and you've registered, you'll have access to your bank account.

A banking session always begins by entering a password to ensure you really are who you claim you are.

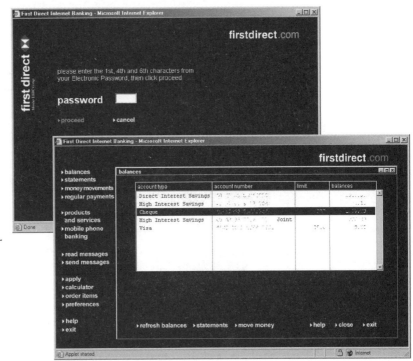

Keep your password safe – it's the key to opening your bank account.

Once you're logged in you will get to the balances page where you can see exactly what you've got (or haven't got) in your accounts.

The First Direct website can be viewed at *www.firstdirect.com/*

There is a link from their home page which will provide you with information about opening a First Direct bank account.

Internet banking has had some bad press, unfairly in my opinion. Stories abound about hackers intercepting individuals' bank accounts and moving money, but these stories are largely bogus. Internet banking sites like First Direct are as safe as any traditional banking method. Some would argue that they are safer.

Finance – mortgage

This is another relatively new service which looks set to become very popular. Most people who own a home have a mortgage. The question everyone is asking is 'Am I paying too much?' A visit to *www.moneyextra.com/* could provide you with the answer. Within seconds.

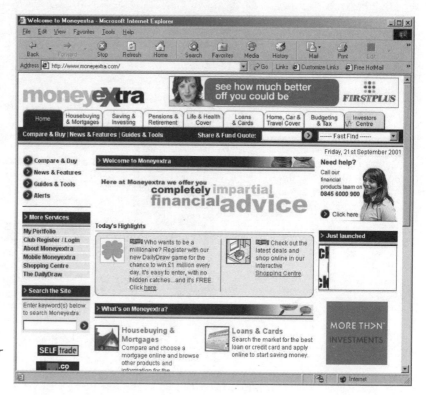

To get the full benefit of this service, register first.

From the home page, there are links to help you calculate what you should be paying for your mortgage. You'll be required to enter some basic details about your home and the length of mortgage remaining and within a very short space of time, a response will come back telling you if it's worth changing your mortgage lender.

Every variation of mortgage is considered and all from the comfort of your own home.

This type of service is likely to become more widespread over the next few years.

Ordering a credit card

As if to endorse the security of the Internet, one major finance company is offering a credit card which can only be ordered over the Internet.

Egg launched their plastic card at the end of 1999 and offers users a 2% discount in interest on purchases made on the Internet.

If you intend doing a lot of shopping on the Internet, this could be the best credit card to hold.

When you log onto *www.egg.com/* you can visit the card-ordering page and complete all of your application details online.

You will then be given an immediate response as to your recommended credit limit. If you agree, the card will be sent, usually within 7 to 10 working days.

Using your card

Internet shopping can only work if you have a credit card, or some sort of arrangement whereby vendors can be paid electronically. But people are reluctant to give away their credit card details to a machine that will transmit its details halfway round the world.

And can you blame them? Contrary to what some might have you believe, the Internet is not a bombproof fortress. There have been numerous examples of fraud carried out on the Internet, and as quickly as one hole is plugged, another seems to gape open.

But let's get it into perspective. Users of credit cards are notoriously lax in their everyday 'conventional' (i.e. non-Internet) business.

When we buy goods at a shop counter and pay with a credit card, frequently the salesperson doesn't even bother to check that the signatures on the card and on the receipt are the same. We can all cite examples when we could have signed the slip 'Donald Duck' and nobody would have noticed. And what do we do with the receipt which contains, amongst other things, our credit card number and expiry date? Walk out of the shop and chuck it on the floor. Wander around any supermarket car park and you're sure to find someone's credit card details on a discarded till receipt. Make sure they're not yours.

Your credit card company will insure you against loss for most high-value transactions.

You have a meal in a restaurant and pay with a credit card. The waiter takes your card and disappears into a dark corner with it for several minutes. What's he doing? Probably what he should be doing, but you wouldn't be the first to have your credit card details copied by a 'here-today-gone-tomorrow' waiter to provide someone with the data to forge your card or use the number to buy goods over the phone or Internet.

Credit card forgery is a huge problem in everyday life. Probably the safest place to use your plastic is on the Net, providing you take sensible precautions.

Precautions

The following precautions should keep you safe:

1. Do not buy from anyone other than a reputable outlet. Giving away your credit card details to a backstreet outfit run by a couple of characters of dubious background is asking for trouble. If what you want to buy is legitimate, buy it from a legitimate outlet.

2. Avoid buying from overseas companies. It's not that they're dishonest, it's just that if something does go wrong it's that much harder to sort it out if the other party is on the other side of the world and doesn't even speak the same language.

3. Only give your credit card details over a secure connection. There is a small chance of someone intercepting your card details over a non-secure connection, but a secure connection is far safer. You'll know when you switch from a secure to a non-secure connection (and vice versa) because a message will appear on the screen.

 Also look out for the padlock symbol at the bottom of your browser, and https instead of http in the web address.

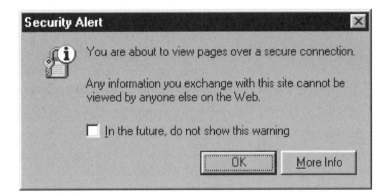

 You do have the option of preventing the warning appearing when you change between secure and insecure connections. This is not to be recommended.

4. Never send credit card details via email. Email is not a secure service and is easily intercepted. If the company you wish to purchase from is worthwhile purchasing from, they will have a secure service. If they haven't, buy elsewhere. Even sending part of the number with one mailing and the rest with another mailing is not wise.

What will the future bring?

In this business, crystal ball gazing is not to be recommended. Not only is the technology moving very rapidly, it also changes direction very rapidly. A concept which may be on the horizon today may never come to fruition because something else has rendered it obsolete whilst still unborn.

Ordering the weekly food on the Internet can save a considerable amount of time, but it is not always easy to find what you're looking for and then the time you would have spent going to the shop is spent instead sitting in front of a computer. When I visit my local supermarket personally, I always pick up a couple of cartons of fresh juice. I always buy the same and I recognise it from the size of the container, its weight (by 'feel' rather than a known quantity) and colour. I have a vague notion of what it might cost, but that's about it. Trying to pick that particular product online from a written list of 20 other similar products was so difficult that I resorted to raiding the dustbin to retrieve the old carton so that I could copy the description.

Read Chapter 7 on Interaction.

The major development will be in the quality of software which we will use to shop. Picking products from a list is not satisfactory, but virtual reality 3D shopping is already available and just around the corner. Once online, you push your virtual shopping trolley up and down virtual aisles and pick products from virtual shelves. It's much easier, far more friendly and when that technology becomes widespread, then e-commerce will really take off.

But to download that type of software so that it will run at a sensible speed needs faster lines of communication. In other words, you're not going to get real-time virtual reality down a conventional telephone line.

The day is fast approaching when we will all need digital phone lines.

See me, hear me

It's possible to send more than just plain text over the Internet. This chapter shows how you can send voice messages, and both still and moving pictures.

Covers

Chapter Nine

What do you need?

Transmitting sound and graphics (both still and moving) is not as difficult as you might think and doesn't require a great deal of expensive equipment.

In addition to the usual multimedia kit, you'll need a method of inputting sound and a method of capturing video.

Sound

Sound is easy to organise and is very cheap. All you need is a microphone which connects into your sound card. Most sound cards have an input port which is in the form of a 3.5mm stereo jack socket which the microphone should be plugged into. The microphone then either sits on your desk or attaches to the side of your monitor.

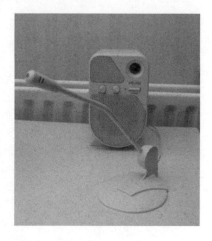

Video

This is a little trickier and slightly more expensive, although not as much as one might think. There are professional video conferencing kits on the market which cost about the same as a top quality desktop PC, but for home use that shouldn't be necessary.

If your computer has a USB port, try and get a video camera which plugs into it, rather than using the parallel port.

You can get excellent results from one of the small web cameras which sit on top of your monitor.

There are at least a dozen to choose from. They're all roughly the same price and have roughly the same features.

The quality, whilst not up to top video conferencing quality, is excellent and belies its low price.

The kits are provided with software which must be installed, but setup is usually then quite straightforward.

For laptop computers, there are small cameras which connect into the PCMCIA socket.

If you have a video camcorder then you may be able to use this as an alternative. If you choose this route, you'll need a video capture card (which will plug into your computer) into which you'll need to connect the camcorder. This solution may give slightly better results, but will not be any cheaper as the cost of a good video capture card is about the same price as a webcam kit which includes all the software needed to set it up and run it.

Some webcams also include the software required to operate a video phone. Generally the results are at least as good as, and frequently better than, 'real' video phones.

Of course to really get the full benefit of this technology you need at least one friend who has similar kit. If you can organise this, you'll find that experimenting with video conferencing, even on a budget, is an exciting and rewarding area of the Internet.

Voice email

The rise in modem speeds has meant that you can now send much larger files across the Internet. One of the more recent developments has been voice email.

There are several programs capable of recording and then sending the recordings, but the easiest is Voice E-Mail by Bonzi.

The program is available free from Bonzi's website at: *www.bonzi.com/* as a limited use evaluation version. If you like it, you can purchase and download the full version.

When the program has been installed and run, a small toolbar will be displayed in the top right corner of the screen. To create a message, click on the Create button.

This opens the window in which you can create your voice email:

If you have a digital camera or webcam you can include a picture and that will be sent as well.

Creating the message is a simple matter of entering the email address of the recipient and speaking into the microphone to record your message.

Receiving voice email

The recipient collects their email in the usual way, with the normal email program (probably Outlook Express or Netscape Messenger). Among the new messages will be the following:

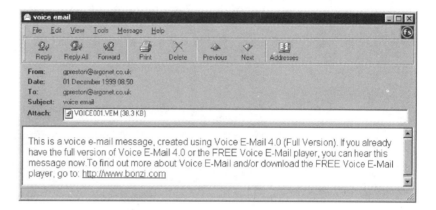

The voice message will be included as an attachment. The text message is automatically generated to tell the recipient the s/he will need Voice E-Mail to read it.

When the recipient has installed Voice E-Mail (either the evaluation version or the full version) they will be able hear your message and, if you included a picture, see who sent it.

The recipient doesn't need to buy the program to hear your message as there is a free reader on Bonzi's website.

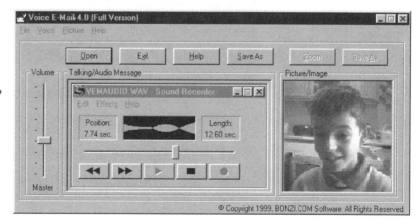

Video email

The next best thing to sending a voice email is to send a video email. Logitech's web camera comes with a very versatile program that allows you to record a short film and email it.

Sending a video email

All of the video email programs are slightly different, but most require just three steps:

1 Click on the Video icon and begin recording your video.

Video uses up lots of memory. You won't be able to email a feature length film.

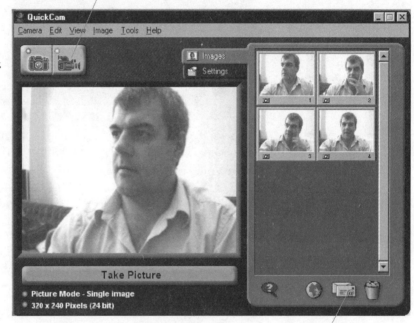

Place the camera so that you can look straight into it. That way, the recipient will think you're talking to them.

2 When you've completed it you can review it, and when you're happy with it, click the Email icon.

3 You'll then be asked to enter the email address of the recipient.

As soon as you're ready to send it, the program will connect you to the Internet and send it.

Receiving a video email

When the recipient next downloads his email, there will be a message generated by the computer, with your movie file attached. Outlook Express displays a paper clip in the top right of the message, and clicking on it will give the recipient the opportunity of either playing it or saving it.

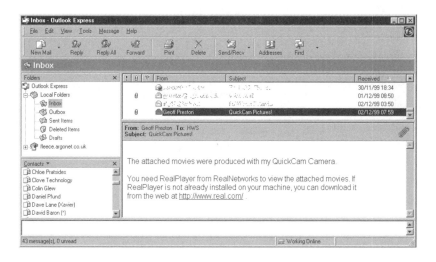

It's worth downloading Real Player even if you don't anticipate playing video emails.

To play the message the recipient must have Real Player which is a free download from *www.real.com/*

Live video

The ultimate development is to send and receive live video simultaneously. This is called video conferencing.

Hardware

This demonstration was set up on opposite sides of the same room, but the computers could have been on opposite sides of the world.

To do any serious video conferencing you need some fairly expensive kit, which is purpose-designed to enable you to have a meeting with several others who could be on opposite sides of the world. If, however, you have a camera and a microphone, you probably will have everything you need to operate a modest conference. In fact, you can manage without the camera – but that will mean that the other person will not be able to see you.

Software

If you have Internet Explorer 6, then you have Microsoft NetMeeting and this will be adequate for most people's needs at home.

NetMeeting is straightforward to set up and comes with excellent on-screen help to guide you through the setup procedure.

With NetMeeting, you can see and hear the person you're talking to, and they can see and hear you, but live. The video frames are a little jumpy but considering how much data is being transmitted and received, it's pretty good.

Even very young children can use this technology.

This program also features an interactive whiteboard which both parties can share.

This technology will become more widespread during the next few years, particularly in education where children will be able to hold conversations with other children in this country and overseas. And all for the cost of a local telephone call.

Webcams

A webcam can be set up to automatically generate pictures at regular intervals providing a continuously updating sequence of pictures. In effect, time-lapse photography with frames being updated at intervals of anything between a few seconds and several minutes.

A visit to *www.liveviews.org/* will provide a list of many of the webcams throughout the world.

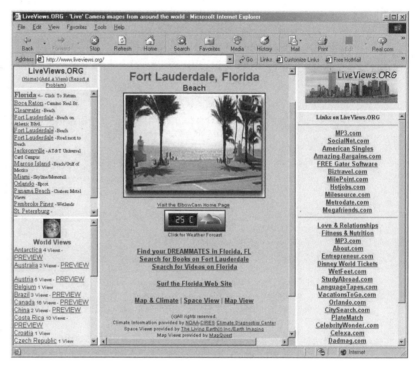

If you're planning a visit, check to see if there's a local webcam so you can see what the weather is doing.

Apart from the fact that it can be fun watching people at work and play in far-off exotic lands, there is a practical use too. If you're making a journey, for example, a webcam can show you exactly how much traffic there is. It can also show what the weather is like at a particular location.

Even more fun than watching a webcam, is setting up your own.

Your own webcam

If you've got a webcam, then you can set it up so that it takes a series of pictures which are then uploaded one at a time to a website.

In addition to a webcam, you'll need a website to send the image to and a good phone connection. If you're going to try this, you can get good results with a dial-up connection, but for best results you should consider a digital or broadband connection which is explained on page 172.

Liveviews.org also provides valuable information about how you could set up your own webcam.

Logitech's webcam (shown on page 144) is supplied with software which will automatically take pictures at pre-set intervals. When the picture has been taken the software sends it to a website, over-writing the picture previously sent there.

All you will now need to do is set the webpage to automatically refresh at the same rate as pictures are sent to the website so that anyone viewing the page will always see the latest picture.

If you're not familiar with webpage construction, see Chapter 13.

Immediately after the webpage title add the line:

<META HTTP-EQUIV="refresh" CONTENT="30">

to make the page refresh (in this case every 30 seconds). In the place you want the picture to appear add:

<IMG SRC="pic.jpg" HEIGHT="144" WIDTH="176">

where *pic.jpg* is the name of the picture.

Music on the web

This chapter shows you how to get music from the Internet, how to use it and how to use the Internet to catalogue your CD collection.

Covers

Chapter Ten

Introduction

If you like to listen to music by a particular group, singer or composer, the chances are you'll go to your local music shop and buy a plastic disc containing recordings of your chosen music. It will come in a special protective case, probably with pictures and information about the artist. The shop will carefully wrap your purchase and you'll pay for it before trundling back home to insert it into a special player.

The only variation with this activity in recent years has been the change from black discs (vinyl records) to silver discs (Compact Discs).

Since the advent of affordable record players, this is how we have collected and played our favourite music. But getting music you like doesn't have to be like this, and if some people have their way, it won't be for much longer.

Although theoretically not as good as CDs, in reality few people can tell the difference.

The current trend is towards music files called MP3. These are computer files of digital recordings which can be downloaded from the Internet and played on your computer. Previously, digital recordings stored as computer files used copious quantities of disc space and clearly were not really suitable for downloading from the Internet. The average track on a Compact Disc is about 35Mb.

MP3 recordings are much smaller but as far as the average person is concerned, no less perfect. This is because they have been created with all the sounds that humans can't hear removed. This reduces them to about one-tenth of their original size which works out at just over 1Mb per minute of music. The average song track is about 3 minutes which translates to about 3–3.5Mb which doesn't take too long to download, but the quality is still excellent.

Personally I can't tell the difference between a CD on my hi-fi and MP3 on my computer.

To get the full value of digital sound on your computer you'll need a good sound card and very good speakers. Most multimedia computers are sold with only a passable sound card, and speakers that often aren't up to even that standard. But these will be good enough to get you going.

Ideally you need a 32-bit sound card and good quality mains-powered and amplified stereo speakers, preferably with a sub-woofer to really bring the sound alive. Anything less will produce sound which is less pure, but still very acceptable.

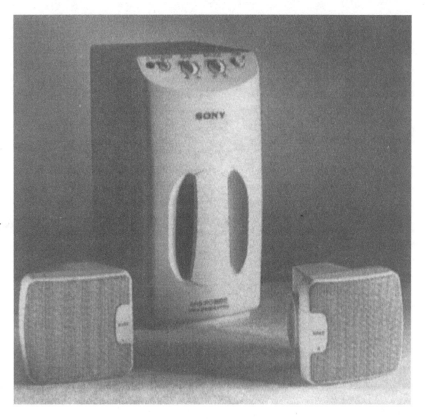

If you're going to get seriously involved with MP3, buy a good sound card and speakers.

To download the MP3 files, you really do need a fast modem otherwise is will take a long time.

You'll also need a credit card because many of the songs are chargeable. Many are free, but it seems that all the songs that have ever been heard of, by artists that are anything more than vaguely familiar, require to be paid for, although the cost can work out much less than you think.

Where do I get MP3 files?

There are several sites from which you can download files, but one of the most popular is Lycos Music which is at *music.lycos.com/ mp3/*

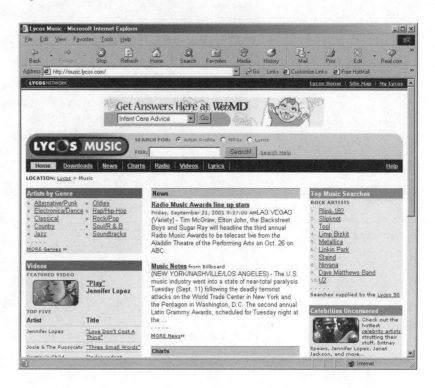

MP3 is the most widely searched for word – even more than sex.

At Lycos Music you can search for MP3 recordings by either song name or artist name. The library is huge and is getting larger by the hour.

It's also worth investigating *mp3.box.sk/* which has a list of all the best MP3 search engines.

Do not get involved with illegal files; pay for legitimate ones.

Other legitimate MP3 sites exist, but so do several less legitimate ones. Some sites contain huge quantities of pirated music which is either being sold off cheap or given away.

These should be avoided at all costs, as should individuals who attach MP3 files to news postings or to emails.

Although not strictly an Internet item, this is a useful accessory for

MP3 fans.

Another way of getting MP3 files is to copy them from your own music CDs using CD ripper software.

Many of the MP3 sites include CD ripper software or provide links to other sites which have it. These are programs that will read a recording on a music CD and convert it into an MP3 file. There are lots available either free or for a small fee.

You simply place your music CD into your CD ROM drive in your PC and run the software. You choose a track to rip and the program creates an MP3 file from it (usually faster than real time).

Be aware of the laws on copyright.

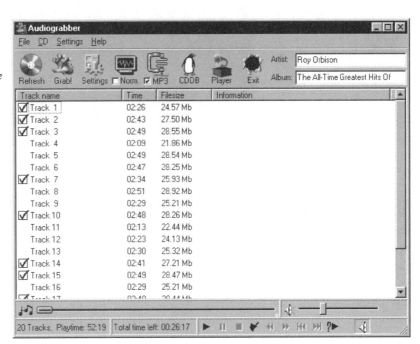

Audiograbber is one of the best and is available from Tucows' website at: *www.tucows.com/*

Note
Copying recordings is illegal. Strictly, it's illegal to copy tracks from Compact Discs onto cassette tape, Mini Disc or MP3 files for your own use. It's really a very serious offence to convert tracks from Compact Discs into MP3 format and distribute them over the Internet.

What do I need to play MP3 files?

All you need to play MP3 files on your computer is a software MP3 player, of which there are several and mostly free.

Top of the list must be Sonique which is distributed free by Lycos and can be found at *www.sonique.com/*

Sonique can be displayed in three different sizes, but only the largest version gives access to all of the features.

Sonique can also play web radio.

Sonique has several displays including information about the current track and a graphical output of the music being played.

Looking as though it were carved from a solid piece of granite, Sonique does not run in the usual and familiar Microsoft window, but it does behave in much the same way as a window (you can move it around, place it behind other windows etc.).

The controls allow you to play any number of tracks and there is scope for repeating tracks as well as skipping.

The audio enhancement panel provides scope for setting the balance and the speed and pitch of the playback.

MP3 files that have previously been downloaded and saved onto your computer can be dragged from windows into Sonique and played through your computer's sound system.

Although you can use previously downloaded MP3 files with Sonique, this program will log onto the Internet and search for particular files if you wish. This is generally a better way of downloading and importing files as Sonique can do it all in one operation.

Sonique can connect to the Internet and download MP3 files for you.

Once you have amassed your collection of MP3 files you can 'tell' Sonique where they are and they will be played whenever you run Sonique. The songs can be changed around just as you would do with CDs or Mini Discs.

If Sonique is too gimmicky, then try Xing's MP3 player which is also free as part of their CD ripper software, AudioCatalyst.

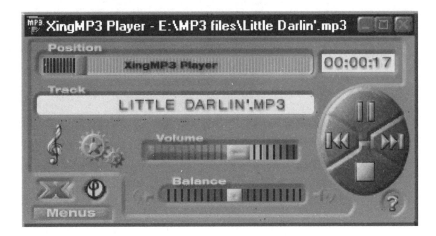

Xing's MP3 player is much more straightforward, although it doesn't have all of the features of Sonique.

The limited use, but free, AudioCatalyst, together with Xing's MP3 player, can be obtained from Xing's website at: *www.xingtech.com/*

If you like the CD ripper, there's a small charge for the fully working version.

Web radio

Music while you work takes on a whole new meaning with radio coming through the Internet whilst you are using your computer.

Several radio stations provide this service and logging onto a radio station website provides a great deal of additional information about the programmes and presenters whilst also providing the same music as can be heard on the radio.

You'll need a good set of speakers to get good quality music.

Internet radio enables you to hear a radio station that is out of range for a normal radio receiver.

You'll be asked what type of connection you have and the faster the connection, the better the music quality.

Interestingly, the music arrives up to 30 seconds behind that which comes through the radio. This is because the Internet music may have to pass through several computers before it arrives at yours. In short, it has a longer journey than the radio waves.

Rather than listen to one radio station, you can choose from several by going to *music.lycos.com/radio/*. Lycos Radio takes you to one of the several websites that transmit radio broadcasts via the Internet.

You can also play radio with Sonique.

You can choose from a wide range of channels (in Lycos' case there are over 30) and you're even told what is playing at a particular moment on each of the channels.

You choose the station by clicking on its name and (in the case of Lycos) you will be taken to a setup page where you will need to specify a few important points about the system you're running.

Although the video looks great, it ties up your computer for longer periods.

Once you're in, you can change channels with exactly the same freedom as you can with a conventional radio.

To get the best from this system you need a good Internet connection, preferably a continuous connection rather than a dial-up connection which will generate a large phone bill just for listening to the radio.

Catalogue your CD collection

It's long been known that music Compact Discs can be played on your computer's CD drive. To help with this pursuit there have been countless virtual CD players to enable you to control the tracks and the discs – if you have more than one CD drive.

It then came about that the name of the CD and the track titles could be displayed whilst the music was playing by matching a CD's serial number to a database which the user had to build himself or herself.

Some recordings marketed in certain countries can get confused with similar recordings intended for other countries.

Typing in all of the track titles for even a modest CD collection is a time-consuming task. Not to mention tedious.

The Deluxe CD player supplied with later versions of Windows is not, as many thought, yet another version of the same thing. This player has one fundamental difference. When you insert a music CD that you haven't used before, the program will connect itself to the Internet and access a website that holds a catalogue of music CDs.

This is an excellent way to catalogue your CD collection.

The serial number of the CD will be matched against the database held on the website and, if a match is made, it will download the title of the CD together with the names of the tracks.

In addition to pulling down the CD details, it will, if you choose, connect you to a website that will give you more information about the artist featured on the current CD.

Alternatively, *www.cddb.com/* will supply the full details of the music CD in your drive which can be copied as a text file.

Downloading

There are countless programs on the Internet which can be downloaded and run on your computer. But this chapter is about more than getting free programs. It also covers grabbing text and graphics from the web.

Covers

Chapter Eleven

Downloading drivers

When you buy a new piece of hardware for your PC (e.g. printers, scanners, modems, sound cards), it will come with driver software. In simple terms, the software 'tells' the computer what the product is, what settings are available and how the computer is to communicate with the hardware.

Always use the latest drivers.

Although the hardware itself doesn't change (until the manufacturer brings out a new model) the software drivers are regularly updated and improved upon. It is usually in the user's best interests to run the latest drivers for their computer hardware and the best place to get the latest driver is from the manufacturer's website.

All of the top manufacturers have websites on which they store the latest versions of their drivers. In most cases, the upgrades are free. Once you have arrived at the website, look for the link that goes to the section with the latest drivers.

When buying a new piece of hardware, always take note of the manufacturer's website.

Different sites are mapped out in different ways, but in most cases you'll have to carry out the same procedures, although not necessarily in the order outlined here. This commentary is based on Hewlett Packard's site which is a model of clarity and good webpage design.

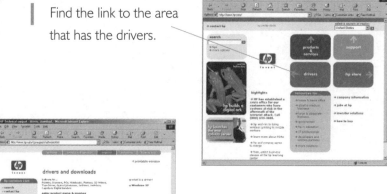

I Find the link to the area that has the drivers.

Make sure you know the exact make and model of the hardware.

2 Specify the type of product (printer, scanner etc.) and the model number.

3 At some point you'll be asked to specify the language for the driver...

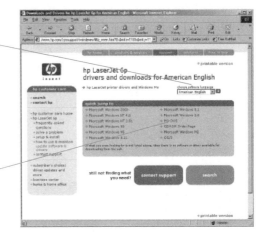

4 ... and the operating system you are using.

Even though this software is provided free, copyright laws still apply.

5 After a final check, click the Download Now button to begin downloading the new driver.

Many companies provide their drivers in two forms – either as a single large file or as a number of smaller files, each of which will save onto one high density floppy disc.

If the driver is intended only to be used on the computer which is being used to download it, select the single large file. If you want to use it on another computer, choose the multiple smaller files and transfer them onto floppy discs when you've downloaded them.

6 A dialog will open offering the choice of either saving the program or running it. Choose Save... then click OK.

Downloads usually come as compressed self-extracting files. Double-clicking them will decompress them and begin installation.

7 A dialog will open giving you the chance to choose a location. The filename determined by the manufacturer will be visible in the Name: window. Change this to something more meaningful if you wish then click Save.

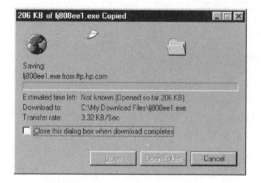

8 The file will now download and the window will show you the current status.

When it's finished downloading, go to the file and double-click on it. It will then unpack itself and begin installing.

Saving webpages

If you want to learn how webpages are written, you could view the source.

Everything that can be viewed on a webpage can be captured either for future reference or to be included in a document of your own.

Webpages in their entirety can be saved, but frequently the page doesn't re-display exactly the same. This is because the pictures are often not included.

Including pictures and diagrams in your documents no longer requires that you buy expensive products like a digital camera or scanner.

1 Go to File at the top left of the screen.

2 Click Save As.

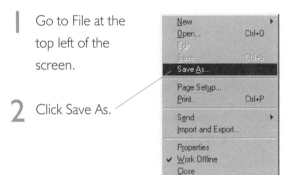

Saving pictures

Unless a clever blocking system has been employed, any picture or icon displayed on a webpage can be saved and, in most cases, used in another document.

1 With the mouse pointer over a picture you wish to save, click the right mouse button to display a menu.

If you do use this feature, always quote the source of the material in your work. It's not reasonable to pinch someone's efforts and pass them off as your own.

2 From the menu, select Save Image As... or Save Picture As...

3 A standard Save dialog will be displayed in which you can choose the name and destination of the file. Clicking on the Save button will save the picture.

Explorer 6 displays a small button bar when the mouse pointer is over a saveable or printable image. You can also email the image by clicking on the envelope.

Capturing text

The easiest way to capture text is to use the copy and paste facility.

This works in exactly the same way with both browsers. Text can be pasted into virtually every program that supports text.

1 Mark the section of text on the webpage that you wish to use by dragging the mouse pointer over the text whilst holding down the left mouse button.

2 Press Ctrl+C to copy the text into an area of the computer's memory called the Clipboard.

3 Open the document you wish to put the copied text into and, with the cursor in the place you wish to place the text, click the left mouse button.

Sometimes web designers force a new line by using a Return. This can have strange effects when the text goes into another document. Use delete to remove unwanted Returns.

4 Paste the text by pressing Ctrl+V

Alternative Internet

In this chapter you can learn about some of the alternative ways to get online.

Covers

Chapter Twelve

You don't need a computer

The majority of Internet users will connect via a desktop computer. If you don't have a desktop computer there are some alternatives.

Set top box

A TV screen is not as good as a monitor for viewing text.

Digital television which is piped into homes frequently comes with numerous interactive goodies including email and Internet. In almost all cases, the email is exactly the same as you would get with a desktop computer connected to an ISP. You can send emails from the TV to a person who usually connects using a computer and vice versa. In many cases, the web facility provided is not full Internet and you will only have access to a few selected pages.

If you choose this method to use the Internet and email, you'll need to invest in a QWERTY keyboard to enter text rather than relying on the remote control supplied with your digital TV connection.

If you want to send emails from your TV you must get a remote control QWERTY keyboard.

Internet TV

At least one television manufacturer has developed a television with Internet connectivity built in. This 'all-in-one' solution requires you to connect both an aerial and a telephone cable into the back of the set so that you can either view TV or surf the net. Whilst this is full Internet access, you won't be able to download and save pictures, text or software as there are no facilities to add additional hardware such as a disc drive. However, this is an extremely effective system providing the user with a TV with email and Internet access in one ready to run unit.

A visit to *www.bush-Internet.com/indexhelp.html* will provide more information about Internet TV.

Games consoles

Sega began a new trend when they announced a new Internet-capable games machine. Following on from the success of their previous games console, the Dreamcast has a built-in modem so that you can access the Internet. The kit includes a lead to connect it to a phone point and a CD ROM containing Internet access software.

An infrared QWERTY keyboard is available at extra cost, but this would be an absolute requirement if you were considering using the console for email or online chat.

Other companies have followed Sega's lead and also provide Internet access with their games consoles.

Is it better?

All of these Internet solutions (and others not mentioned here) are excellent alternatives to using a computer to access the Internet, as long as you recognise that each has its own limitations. These limitations sometimes relate to speed, the amount of Internet access available or the ability to download and save pictures or text. Most of all, you won't be able to carry out all the other tasks normally associated with a computer.

Faster connection

So far, this book has dealt with the most common method of accessing the Internet: a desktop computer and a dial-up connection using a modem and an analogue telephone line. For the majority of cases, this is adequate although it does have four distinct drawbacks:

- it's relatively slow, even with the fastest modem available

- at busy times, you may have to wait before getting a connection

- whilst in use, the phone line is tied up

- when you're on line you're running up a phone bill

You don't need a modem if you have a digital phone line.

Alternatives include a digital line (ISDN – Integrated Services Digital Network) which combines telephone and data enabling voice and Internet to be used simultaneously, and Broadband which uses a special device called a cable modem which transfers data at about 10 times the speed of a conventional modem. Different systems are available in different areas but each overcomes many of the associated problems. They're very much faster, they provide a permanent connection and they don't use the phone line. Of course there is a charge for using an ISDN or a Broadband line but it's usually a flat charge. In other words you pay the same each month regardless of how much you use it.

For more information about these services, visit *www.bt.com* or *www.blueyonder.co.uk/*

Satellite Connection

If you really want to set the world on fire, or you consider ISDN too slow or too outdated, then why not try using a satellite connection. Kits to connect to a satellite are becoming much more affordable. Basically they comprise a card to plug into your computer and a monthly subscription charge of about 3 times that of an Internet account. But, you get a connection claimed to be up to 5 times faster than ISDN.

For more details, including checking if a satellite footprint covers your area, visit *www.satweb.co.uk/*

Do-it-yourself

Most ISPs provide webspace for you and your family to use. Many people don't bother, but creating a family website can be a great deal of fun as well as being a valuable skill to learn. This chapter shows you how to get started.

Covers

Chapter Thirteen

Your own website

As outlined in the introduction, anyone can join the World Wide Web and many Internet Service Providers not only make it easy, but positively encourage it.

Of the 15 free ISPs used to research this book, all gave at least 5 Mb of web space free, and some gave as much as 20 Mb. A couple of years ago there was a significant charge for even 5 Mb of web space. For most people, this is more than enough to create their personal website.

How it works

The basic principle is that you create your webpages and test them on your computer. When you are satisfied that they work, you move them to your ISP, from where the rest of the world can access them, as long as they have the address.

Creating a website can be frustrating and time-consuming, but a great deal of fun.

As time goes by, you will want (or need) to update pages, and add pages to your website. This is done on your computer, and these too will be sent to your ISP to become part of your website, after thorough testing.

Don't get over ambitious

Take a quick scan around the Internet and you will see a huge number of very well-constructed pages. Don't think you'll be able to do something as good as these overnight. Some of the commercial sites are maintained by webmasters and webmistresses who spend their whole life creating webpages and apparently do little or nothing else. And they've been doing it for a long time.

However, you can produce some very creditable webpages with relative ease. As you progress you'll be able to incorporate new features into your site.

There are two things which come out of this:

* the standard of a website will be commensurate with the creator's web building ability. As soon as he or she learns a new trick, it will soon be incorporated into the site

* Websites are never finished

What do I need?

You could probably get away with not having to buy anything to create your website. The most important thing you'll need is a program that can generate webpages. This can be done in three ways.

The hard way

You can normally drag and drop a HTML file into a text document window.

Every computer has some sort of text editor which can be used to create webpages. This means that everyone should be able to create a webpage.

Webpages are created using a language called HTML – HyperText Markup Language. You can type the contents of a webpage into the text editor and save it as a HTML document instead of a text document.

Try typing in this program and saving it as *Test.html*:

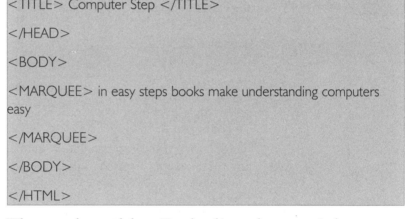

```
<HTML>

<HEAD>

<TITLE> Computer Step </TITLE>

</HEAD>

<BODY>

<MARQUEE> in easy steps books make understanding computers easy

</MARQUEE>

</BODY>

</HTML>
```

'HTML in easy steps' is an excellent introduction to HTML programming.

When you drag and drop *Test.html* into a browser window you should see the title 'Computer Step' on the top left of the window title bar and the words 'in easy steps books make understanding computers easy' scrolling across the screen (assuming your browser supports scrolling text).

An easier way

Many programs will output files as a webpage. Both Microsoft Word and Microsoft Publisher can, but there are several others.

The way to check if a particular program will create webpages is to open a document, click on File on the menu bar at the top of the screen, and look to see if Save as HTML appears in the menu.

If it does, you can use that program to create webpages.

Not everything you do in a word processor will translate into a webpage.

Alternatively, from the File menu, click on Save As... and at the very bottom of the dialog is a panel alongside Save as type. Click on the panel and a menu of possible filetypes will open. Check to see if HTML is

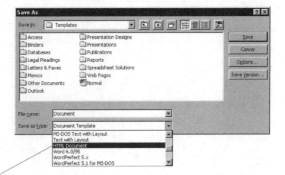

there. If it is, it means that that program can output files in HTML and therefore can be used to generate webpages.

But a word of caution. In most cases, the program you choose to use to output HTML will almost certainly be capable of doing far more than HTML can handle. The result will be that the document you so carefully laid out may not look exactly the same when translated into HTML. In particular, different sections may not sit alongside each other correctly.

The other problem is that most word processors can handle a variety of graphic objects. If using a word processor to create webpages, stick to GIF and JPEG graphics only.

The easiest way

By far the easiest way to create webpages is to use a dedicated webpage designer.

When installing Microsoft's Internet Explorer suite you will have had the option of installing FrontPage Express which is Microsoft's webpage editor.

If you use Netscape Communicator, then you will have Composer as part of the package.

Most of the top websites are created using a variety of tools, including coding raw HTML.

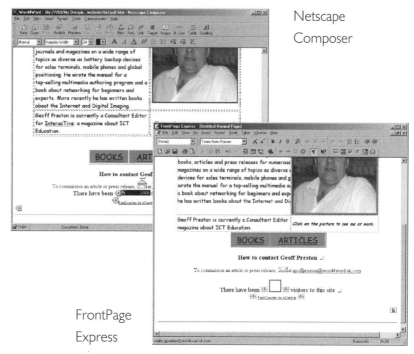

Netscape Composer

FrontPage Express

These programs (and others which can be purchased in addition to these) provide easy access to all of the tools required to make up pages in HTML. They look and operate in much the same way as a document processor such as Word or Publisher, but they won't let you do anything that can't be translated into HTML (a disadvantage of the previous method).

Linking pages

Even if you intend using a special editor, it's worth doing a little experimenting with HTML so you can get a feel of what it can do and how it works.

If you haven't already done so, create a webpage using a text editor as described on page 175. Save it as *Test.html*.

To make alterations to it, drag the file from the filer window into a text document window.

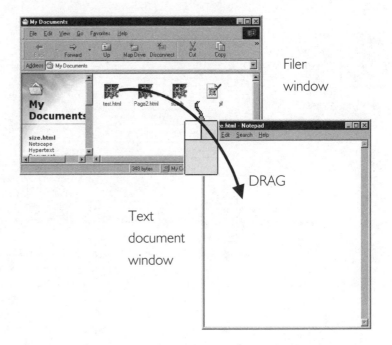

Filer window

Text document window

DRAG

Websites are pages of information which are connected using hyperlinks. This is the part that frightens off most people, but it really isn't difficult to grasp, or to execute.

Having created a simple webpage, drag it into a document window and add the following line immediately before the second from last line:

```
<A HREF="Page2.html">Click here</A>
```

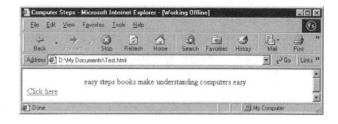

Copy these instructions exactly as they appear here, including the chevrons '<' and '>'.

Next create a new page and enter the following:

```
<HTML>

<HEAD>

<TITLE> Page Two </TITLE>

</HEAD>

<BODY>

<P> This should be another page.

</P>

<A HREF="Test.html"> Return to 1st page</A>

</BODY>

</HTML>
```

These two pages hardly constitute a website, but this is the basis upon which all websites are created.

Save this document as *Page2.html*.

Now, when you drop *Test.html* into your browser, you should see an underlined link under the scrolling text. Clicking on this link should open the second document which should contain an underlined link which will return you to the first page.

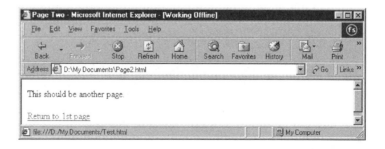

Pretty text

The text used previously will be fine, although it will be all the same colour and all the same size.

Text colour

Text colour is determined by stating the quantities of red, green and blue. These numbers are quoted using a strange numbering system called hexadecimal. Put simply, it uses numbers 0 to 9 and then letters A to F.

Placing:

You must use COLOR and not COLOUR.

```
<FONT COLOR="#FFFFFF">
```

will change the following text to white. Whilst:

```
<FONT COLOR="#000000">
```

will change it to black.

Each pair of digits represents each of the colours red, green and blue in that order so:

```
<FONT COLOR="#FF0000">
```

will give pure red, whilst:

```
<FONT COLOR="#00FF00">
```

will give pure green, and:

If each pair of digits is the same, you'll get a shade of grey.

```
<FONT COLOR="#0000FF">
```

gives pure blue.

You can mix colours and you can use different quantities of each colour so that:

```
<FONT COLOR="#AA0088">
```

gives a sort of purple, and:

```
<FONT COLOR="#44AACC">
```

gives a rather fetching shade of sky blue.

Text size

To change the text size, use the command:

`<FONT SIZE=n>`

where *n* is a number between 1 and 7.

Use the larger size for titles only.

Using the command:

`</FONT>`

changes the font size back to what it was before it was last changed.

Font style

If the person looking at your page doesn't have the font you specified, the page may not be displayed properly.

You can change the style of the font (the typeface) using:

`<FONT FACE = "fontname">`

where *fontname* is the name of the font.

Adding a picture

Sooner or later you will want to add some graphics to your webpages. The instruction is:

Initially, the safest way is to keep the document and the picture together.

```
<IMG SRC="name.gif">
```

where *name*.gif is the filename of a picture, including the three digit DOS suffix. The picture should be placed in the same filer window as the HTML document or it must have its location specified as part of the name.

Other useful commands

The list of HTML commands is long, and it's difficult to choose a small number to give a taste of what can be done. Here are some of the most popular:

This is but a small selection of the HTML commands available to you.

<BODY BGCOLOR="#*rrggbb*">	sets the background colour for the whole page.
<HR>	draws a horizontal line across the page
<FONT SIZE=+1>	increases the font size by one
<FONT SIZE=-1>	decreases the font size by one
<P ALIGN="*p*">	aligns text where *p* is either center, left or right
<I>	italicises text
</I>	switches off italics
<B>	emboldens text
</B>	switches off emboldened text

All commands go between < and >. A slash (/) switches off a previously issued command.

Where to get web resources

The best place to get resources for your website is, unsurprisingly, on the web.

The easiest way to track down these resources is to go to Yahoo (*www.yahoo.com/*) and enter GIF in the search field.

Use the resources that are being freely given away rather than pinching them from someone else's website.

The resulting list provides links to countless sites offering free use of:

animated GIFs	—	little animations
digitised photos	—	quality pictures in the correct format
icons	—	to guide the user around your site.

You should find a great deal of material to enhance your website.

Uploading

Check, check and check again before uploading your website.

When you have completed your webpages and you have tested them thoroughly to ensure that everything works as it should, it must be sent to your Internet Service Provider. This is called uploading.

Different ISPs have slightly different arrangements for uploading. Some ISPs provide their own uploader, whilst others expect you to provide your own. Your ISP will provide you with information about uploading, but in many cases you will be expected to download an FTP suite such as CuteFTP (which is free from

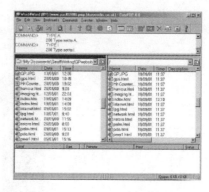

www.cuteftp.com/) or WS_FTP (from *www.ipswitch.com/*) for which there is a small charge.

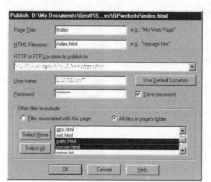

Even the slightest alteration means that the relevant page(s) will need to be uploaded again.

Alternatively you could use the uploader which is part of the editor you are using to create your website.

Either way, you'll need to check a few things with your ISP before you can upload. You may already have been supplied with the information, but you will usually need to know the name of the first page of your website. (This might be *home.html* or *index.html* or something similar.) You'll need to know your upload password and the address to which you must send your web files. You'll also need to know your URL – the Internet address you'll need to enter to access your website from anywhere in the world.

You may have to choose which pages you want uploaded. The first time it will be all of them, but from then you will only need to upload pages that have been changed or new pages added.

Advertising your site

Tell your friends about your website first.

For some, just building a modest website is sufficient and they don't feel the need to advertise it, nor do they feel let down if nobody visits it. But it would be a shame not to share all your hard work with others. Perhaps just close friends, perhaps the whole world.

Before you do announce your creation, put a counter on the front page which records how many people have visited your site. Many ISPs supply one, but if your ISP doesn't, go to one of the many sites that give them free like *www.webcounter.com/* or *www.htmlcounter.com/* and use one of their counters, which includes instructions.

Test your site carefully before announcing it to the world.

Notifying close friends is easy. Email them, and include in your email signature the address of your website. If they are using a modern email program then they will just need to click on the address to be taken there.

Notifying the rest of the world is no less easy with sites such as *www.submit-it.com/*

If your site is on a specific theme, why not join a webring?

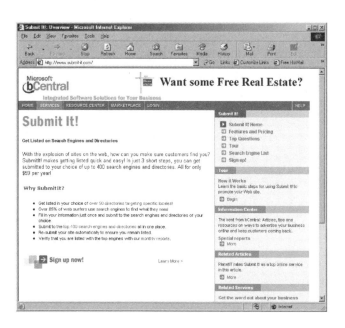

Once you've entered your details (and paid a small fee) details of your site will be sent to a variety of search engines.

What else do I need?

If you have an Internet account with personal web space and you have Internet Explorer or Netscape Communicator then you have everything you actually *need*. With this, all you will be able to do is produce a website with lots of text, illustrated with a few bits of clip art you picked up from here and there.

Icons and buttons

Icons and simple buttons which are personal to you can be produced using a paint program, as long as it will output as a GIF file which is the favoured file format for graphics on the web. There are some programs which will enable you to produce animated icons.

You can spend a small fortune on goodies to enhance your website, but you should not buy them for this purpose alone.

Photos

You will doubtless want to include some pictures, possibly photographs on your website. These can be captured in one of two ways. The more expensive way is to buy a digital camera. Unlike conventional cameras, a digital camera takes pictures and saves them either to disc or to memory within the camera. These pictures can then be transferred to your computer as either a GIF file or a JPEG file. (For pictures, JPEG is generally reckoned to be the better option.)

The cheaper option is to buy a scanner. Flatbed scanners which connect to your computer via either the parallel or (preferably) a USB port are now incredibly cheap. Your old family photographs can then be scanned and dropped into your website. In some respects this is a better buy than the camera as it can be used for so many other things including scanning pages of text and translating them into editable text.

Video

If you have a means of capturing video such as a webcam, you can include small movies on your webpage, but don't go overboard with this feature. They can take a long time to download.

The limitation is your imagination, not your pocket.

Index

M

N

O

P

1–100

There are thousands of websites out there. Some will leave you wondering how you managed without them. Others will leave you wondering why anyone bothered to create them.

Here are some of the best:

1. Accountants

Assoc. of Chartered Certified Accountants

www.acca.co.uk/

Like many modern websites, this one opens with a slick movie. The first time you go to the site, the movie makes an interesting diversion where you can marvel at the ingenuity of the web designer. On subsequent visits the movie just wastes time so look for the link entitled 'Skip Movie'.

Chartered Accountants Directory

www.chartered-accountants.co.uk/

Sometimes, the finances are just so complicated you need somebody else to sort them out for you. If you want to find a chartered accountant, this is the first place to visit.

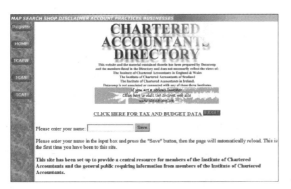

2. Alternative Medicine

Acupuncture-UK

www.acupuncture-uk.co.uk/

Once the butt of musical-hall jokes and TV sitcoms, the ancient Chinese art of sticking needles into various parts of the body to cure specific ailments is rapidly gaining more and more recognition in western medicine.

British Acupuncture Council

www.acupuncture.org.uk/

More information about pins and needles from this UK site.

Creative Changes

www.hypnosis.demon.co.uk/

This company claims to provide a unique and individual service to clients needing help. They supply a range of hypnosis and self-help products, designed to assist you with your area of difficulty.

Guide to Aromatherapy

www.fragrant.demon.co.uk/

Some people claim that different smells can help with a variety of symptoms, including stress-related problems. I don't know about that, but I found many of the aromas very relaxing.

Homeopathy Home Page

www.homeopathyhome.com/

The Queen, I'm told, is a homeopathic user. If you want to find out more about homeopathy, this site is well worth a visit.

Homeopath.co.uk

www.homeopath.co.uk/

Another useful homeopathic site with lots of information about the science.

Hypnosis Online

www.hypnosis.org.uk/

Another mystic art that has inspired countless comedy routines. Does it work? I pass no judgement but a visit to this site might help you to make your mind up.

3. Art Galleries

Art Gallery of New South Wales

www.artgallery.nsw.gov.au/

You don't have to travel the world to visit the top art galleries as many, like this Australian gallery, now have their own website enabling you to bring the art into your home. Of course, it's not really as good as visiting in person, but many of these sites are a close second.

Louvre, The

mistral.culture.fr/louvre

The home of Venus de Milo and other great works of art can be visited without trekking to Paris.

Metropolitan Museum

www.metmuseum.org/

Find out about the works, the lectures and even the souvenirs, as well as taking a virtual tour around this famous New York gallery.

Museum of Modern Art

www.moma.org/

Is it art, or is someone having a laugh? The website of Museum of Modern Art enables you to answer the question before visiting something that you may feel is an enormous practical joke.

National Gallery

www.nationalgallery.org.uk/

London's National Gallery houses one of the greatest collections of European paintings in the world.

National Portrait Gallery

www.npg.org.uk/

To get the most from the real gallery, visit this superb website first.

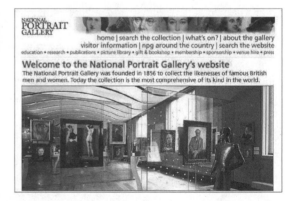

Online Art Gallery

www.artandparcel.com/

Not so much an art gallery but a site to buy new original artwork online.

Tate Gallery

www.tate.org.uk/

The Tate Gallery is one of the most famous galleries in the world. If you are unable to visit the Tate in person (definitely the best idea) then you can always surf there. The site offers a great deal of information about the works on display and has an easy to find index of each artist.

The Turner Prize

www.tate.org.uk/britain/exhibitions/
turnerprize.htm

A cow in formaldehyde and a picture made from elephant droppings are just two of the award winners of the prestigious Turner Prize. Frankly I'm sometimes at a loss to see where the art comes in, but I'm just a simple writer.

4. Auctions

Amazon Auctions

www.amazon.com/

Selling and buying at an auction is great fun, I'm assured. Using an Internet auction is just as much fun and you can bid across the world. If you have something to sell, why not try auctioning it at Amazon?

Auction Guide

www.auctionguide.com/

This is a complete guide to worldwide auctions and includes lots of valuable information about auctioning your surplus items.

Auctions.com

www.auctions.com/

This site enables you to buy and sell all manner of items which are usefully categorised enabling you to get to the items you want without having to wade through the rest.

eHammer

www.ehammer.com/

Register with this auction house and you can buy and sell all manner of goodies.

eBay

www.ebay.com/

This US auction house lists about thirty categories including one category described as 'everything else' which basically mean you can buy and sell anything and everything.

eBid

www.ebid.co.uk/

This UK auction house offers customers the chance to auction items, swap items and co-buy. The latter is a scheme whereby an item is offered for sale at a given price. If, say, five people agree to buy the item, the price is reduced. If ten people agree to buy, the price is reduced still further. In almost all cases you end up paying less than you had originally agreed. A 25% reduction is common, 33% frequent and in some cases, you can save 50% on the initial agreed price.

Also featured is a wanted section where you can advertise for things you'd like, need or want.

Holiday Auctions

www.holidayauctions.com

Rather than wander down to the travel agent, bid for a holiday online. There are some amazing bargains to be had.

Loot

www.loot.com/

The online version of the free paper containing lots of classified ads and an online auction.

QXL

www.qxl.com/

Online spin-off of TV shopping channel offering real-time online bidding in a virtual auction room.

Travelbids

www.travelclearinghouse.com/

More travel bargains available if you don't mind a little uncertainty.

Wine Bid

www.winebid.com/

No prizes for guessing what's on offer here. Use the search engine to find a wine or choose from the list and bid for it.

5. Banking

Barclays

www.barclays.com/

Most major banks have websites and it's worth checking them out from time to time to see who has the best deals for loans and deposits.

HSBC

www.hsbc.co.uk/

As one would expect from a large multinational company, this site is very well organised and contains lots of useful information.

National Westminster

www.natwest.co.uk/

Another high street bank with online facilities enabling you to carry out your financial dealings at any time of the day or night, 365 days a year.

Nationwide

www.nationwide.co.uk/

Building societies are almost a thing of the past as most have now lost their 'mutual' status and are virtually no different from banks in that they offer all the same services.

Of those left, this one stands head and shoulders above the others.

6. Bicycles

Bicycle Helmet Safety Institute

www.bhsi.org/

My first cycle helmet looked like half of a hard boiled egg with the yolk removed. Thankfully modern cycle helmets are much more trendy and should be regarded as a requirement, not an optional extra.

Bicycle Online

www.bicycle.com/

If you want to keep fit and you don't want to contribute to global pollution, what better mode of transport is there than a bike? These amazing contraptions hardly changed for a century but then they acquired suspension, disc brakes, composite frame, hydraulic gears and on-board computers to let you know how far and how fast you're going.

Campagnolo

www.campagnolo.com/

The website of the company that invented the derailleur gear system and patented several other bike related items including the quick-release wheel.

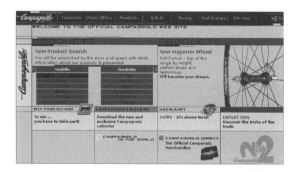

CycleNet

www.cycle-net.org.uk/

Everything the cyclist and cyclist-to-be needs including the bikes themselves at very competitive prices.

Orange Mountain Bikes

www.orangebikes.co.uk/

The bicycle manufacturer famous for its ATBs – All Terrain Bikes.

Peugeot Bicycles

www.peugeot-fietsen.nl/

The website of these quality bike manufacturers gives details about their traditional bikes and their latest mountain machines.

Raleigh

www.raleighbikes.com

The byword for quality UK bikes of all types and for all ages. Learn about the company, their products and where to buy them.

Shimano

www.shimano.com/

This company provides brake and gear components for many top makes, but they also build complete bikes.

ZipCycle

www.zipcycle.com/

If you're tired of cranking your bike uphill, get one of these motor kits to remove some of the legwork.

7. Book Publishers

Addison Wesley Longman

www.awl.com/

When these two companies joined forces they became a formidable force in the publishing world. All titles are listed. If you want to get a book published, there are lots of opportunities.

Book Web

www.bookweb.co.uk/

A popular site featuring links to lots of publishers.

Computer Step

www.ineasysteps.com/

This UK publisher recently celebrated its 10th Anniversary and specialises in computer books for home/business use. The site details all the current and forthcoming books. You can read about the books and buy online via a secure connection.

Puffin

www.puffin.co.uk/

This excellent site details all of their popular children's titles. Also includes details of forthcoming titles, fascinating facts about favourite authors and how a book is made. Orders can be placed online.

Random House

www.randomhouse.co.uk/

Random House, Inc. is the world's largest English-language general trade book publisher. It publishes fiction and non-fiction books by some of the foremost and popular writers of our time.

Stainer & Bell

www.stainer.co.uk/

For almost a century this company has been publishing music and religious books.

Thames and Hudson

www.thameshudson.co.uk/

Search for titles, read about them and buy online.

8. Book Shops

Amazon

www.amazon.com/

www.amazon.co.uk/

Probably the leading online book company offering far more than just a convenient retail facility. You can search for books by title or author, ISBN or genre. There's a section where you can review a book yourself and read reviews by other customers. Look out for discounted items and earn credits to save money on future purchases.

Athena Books

www.athenabooks.demon.co.uk/

The website of the specialist military bookshop. Stock covers 3000 BC–2000 AD and includes Naval, Military and Aviation. Claims to be Europe's largest stockist of antiquarian, new and out of print books.

Blackwell's Bookshops

bookshop.blackwell.co.uk/

The online branch of the famous bookstore has thousands of titles to buy online.

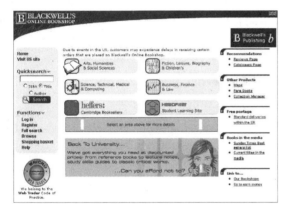

BOL

www.uk.bol.com/

All books are categorised and the search engine makes it easy to find what you're looking for. BOL also sells music and video.

Book Lovers

www.booklovers.co.uk/

Rather than going to a high-street bookshop and having to buy a well-thumbed book, try one of these websites which will sell you a book that's never been touched by browsing shoppers.

Children's Bookshop, The

www.childrensbookshop.com/

Finding books for kids is not always easy. Come here and you'll get lots of ideas and some sound advice.

Church House Bookshop

www.chbookshop.co.uk/

As the name suggests, this company specialises in religious books.

Cooks Book Shop

www.cooks-book-shop.co.uk/

Personally I prefer eating, but if cooking is your forte, this is the place to come for everything connected with food preparation.

Hammicks

www.hammicks.com/

Just like visiting the high street store but without getting out of your armchair.

Just Books

www.justbooks.co.uk/

Unlike some online bookstores, this one doesn't sell videos, DVDs, CDs or computer software.

Technical Book Shop Online

www.techbooks.com.au/

You don't have to be a petrol head or egg head to visit this site, but if you are you'll find it's a superb source for technical books.

Travel Book Shop

www.thomascookpublishing.com/

Maps, guides and tourist information is this company's stock in trade.

Waterstone's Online

www.waterstones.co.uk/

Another famous name with an online branch.

WH Smith

www.whsmith.co.uk/

From its humble beginnings as a newspaper kiosk on railway stations, WH Smith is the high street bookselling giant.

9. Building Services

Acorn Building Services

www.technohelp.org/html/acorn.htm

This company offers a range of services from minor remedial work to major building projects.

Andrew Dodsworth Building Services

www.andrewdodsworth.co.uk/

If it's plumbing, electrical work or central heating installations, look here first. Special features include safety information like the section on Carbon Monoxide.

Emergency Building Services

www.ebs24hr.co.uk/

Hopefully you won't need this site but if you do have a catastrophe they'll be glad to hear from you.

Emergency Electrical Services

www.electricianslondon.co.uk/

There are lots of sites like this covering different parts of the world. This one is for London and features companies offering all kinds of electrical services from installing a door bell to rewiring.

10. Cameras

1st Cameras

www.1stcameras.com/

Learn about cameras, read reviews and buy online.

Best Cameras

www.bestcameras.co.uk/

There are lots of special offers on cameras and accessories to be found on this site.

Cameras Direct

www.camerasdirect.co.uk/

Buy direct from this company and get an unbeatable deal on all photographic equipment.

Canon Cameras

www.canon.co.uk/

The website of the famous manufacturer of film, digital and video cameras.

Digital Camera Company

www.digital-cameras.com/

Digital cameras appear to be overtaking traditional film cameras for everyone but the purists. Although digital cameras are more expensive, the running costs seem to be far less as you only print the ones you want. Whichever camera you prefer, check out the prices on the Internet.

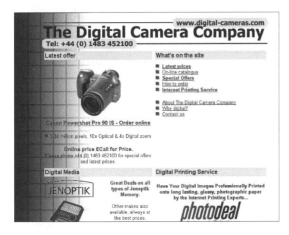

Digital Camera Resource Page

www.dcresource.com/

Everything for the digital camera owner.

Fujifilm – APS Cameras

www.fujifilm.co.uk/consumer/

The Advanced Photo System is so much easier than breaking your finger nails trying to load conventional film cameras. You can even get your snaps printed in one of three formats.

Jessops

www.jessops.com/

Visit a Jessops shop and you'll find yourself talking to someone who knows what they're talking about. Seems obvious, doesn't it? Pity not every shop thinks the same way.

Kodak Limited

www.kodak.co.uk/

Since George Eastman founded Kodak, the name has been a byword for high-quality photographic goods. But there's more to Kodak than rolls of film.

London Camera Exchange

www.lcegroup.co.uk/

Don't throw away your old camera. Take it to the London Camera Exchange and upgrade it to a better model. You'll find lots of second-users photographic items at well below list prices.

Olympus

www.olympus.co.uk/

The website of one of the top camera manufacturers. The Olympus website showcases all their digital cameras, as well as the conventional film models, and also a comprehensive range of accessories.

Pentax

www.pentax.co.uk/

Yet another well-known brand advertising their products online. Visit this site to get all the latest specifications.

11. Camping

British Isles Caravan & Campsite D'base

www.handbooks.co.uk/

Living under canvas is not my first choice for a holiday, but I did once have to spend a night under canvas whilst on a long car journey. Personally I couldn't see the advantage of a tent, especially when the heavens over the Dordogne opened – the noise was indescribable.

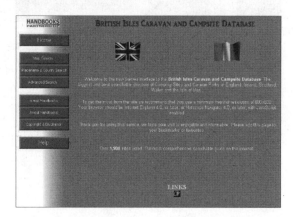

Camping-USA!

www.camping-usa.com/

Having made the journey across the Atlantic, you can see the real USA in a mobile home. A US style camper van is not to be confused with European campers which are little more than converted vans. The Winnebago is like a luxury home on wheels with all the creature comforts of home. This site details places to stop over.

Caravan Club

www.caravanclub.co.uk/

The great British pastime of towing a trailer behind a car is fine until you want to find somewhere to park. The Caravan Club helps with campsites and offers lots of guidance for towing.

Caravan Sitefinder UK

www.caravan-sitefinder.co.uk/

Another site to help find the spot to park the caravan.

Eurocamp

www.eurocamp.co.uk/

This company has sites all over the world. You don't have to hire a tent, you can book a mobile home which is a large trailer, fully plumbed in.

Jackson's Outdoor Leisure Supplies

www.jacksons-camping.co.uk/

If you're determined to sample life in the great outdoors, it's better to be properly equipped. If you're planning a break in the UK or North Europe, you'd better include an umbrella.

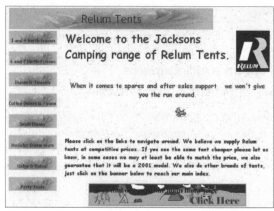

UK Sites Directory

www.uk-sites.com/

A comprehensive Internet directory of caravan parks and camp sites throughout the UK. Simply click the area of the UK you're interested in visiting and get a list of sites.

12. Car Hire

Australia Car Rentals

www.atn.com.au/carhire.htm

Sometimes it's better to use someone else's car than use your own. Sometimes it's simply not practical to take your car. When visiting the other side of the world, for example.

African Car Hire

www.natron.net/tour/ach

Another good reason for not taking your own car on holiday is if the terrain is so rough that it would be pointless attempting to bring it back again.

Alamo Rent A Car

www.goalamo.com/

This US company provides unlimited mileage cars across the US.

Avis Rent A Car

www.avis.co.uk/

You can book a car online at the website of one of the most famous names in vehicle hire.

Car Hire 4 Less

www.carhire4less.co.uk/

Discounted worldwide car rental with leading car rental companies.

Classic Car Hire

www.cornwallclassiccarhire.co.uk/

If you've ever yearned for an exotic car, don't buy one, hire one. There's several to choose from and all at reasonable rates.

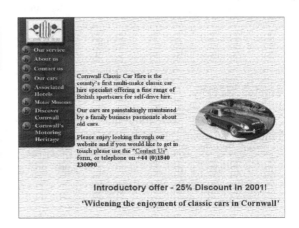

Cornwall Classic Car Hire is the county's first multi-make classic car hire specialist offering a fine range of British sportscars for self-drive hire.

Our cars are painstakingly maintained by a family business passionate about old cars.

Please enjoy looking through our website and if you would like to get in touch please use the "Contact Us" form, or telephone on +44 (0)1840 230090

Introductory offer - 25% Discount in 2001!

'Widening the enjoyment of classic cars in Cornwall'

Craven Classic Car Hire

www.yorkshirenet.co.uk/visinfo/ccch

If you want to create an impression at a job interview, turn up in a classic car hired from this company.

Hertz Rent A Car

www.hertz.co.uk/

Another famous name in rentals offering customers the option of collecting a car from one place and leaving it somewhere else.

Holiday Autos

www.holidayautos.co.uk/

Get 5% off when you book your holiday car online.

National Car Rental

www.nationalcar.com/

Pick a car, a collection point and a place to leave it and book online with this famous car hire company. Full details, including prices and passenger/luggage accommodation, are given for the US/Canadian fleet and the European fleet.

Northern Sports Car Hire

www.sportscarhire.net/

The trouble with a sports car is that it's expensive and you don't use it very often. An alternative is to let someone else have the expense of owning it whilst you simply hire it for a few days a year.

Rent A Wreck

www.rent-a-wreck.com/

This US outfit rent out the scruffiest cars I've ever seen. They're dirty, rusty and bashed up. Body parts frequently don't match, but the cars are safe. When one customer asked where the ashtray is, the reply was, "Honey, the whole car's the ashtray."

Thrifty Car Rental

www.thrifty.co.uk/

Not only cheap car hire, but cheap van hire. It's well worth considering this company when making plans to send one of the kids off to university.

Triple R Luxury Car Hire

www.tripler-clique.com.au/

Choose from the selection of classic European cars like Rolls Royce, Bentley and Jaguar for that special occasion. They will even provide a photographer.

13. Car Imports

All Car Imports

www.all-car-imports.co.uk/

This independent broker specialises in UK car imports. They locate the cheapest deals and put you in direct contact with the European source. Tell them what car you want and the specification and they find the cheapest prices. You pay the European dealer and All Car Imports a small commission.

American Car Imports

www.americancarimports.co.uk/

You can import one of those huge gas-guzzlers, but there are lots of American cars that are more suitable for European roads.

Caldermore Japanese Imports

www.caldermore.co.uk/

Beware of some companies offering imported Japanese cars. They are cheap, but the history isn't always known and many are wrecks which have literally been pulled from scrap yards because of the high cost of keeping 3 year old cars on the streets of Japan.

Carbusters

www.carbusters.com/

It's now well documented that buying a new car in the UK is an expensive business. Buying a car overseas and importing it into the UK can save up to 20% of the purchase price. On a £20,000 car, that's quite a saving. Little wonder so many companies have sprung up to make it even easier to buy cheaper cars.

Car Import Solutions

www.carimportsolutions.co.uk/

Another chance to bring a European sourced car into the UK.

Car Importing From Europe

www.carimporting.co.uk/

If you want to import a car yourself without using a broker, this site tells you how it's done.

Car-prices.com

www.car-prices.com/

This What Car? recommended site lists some of the top bargains. But beware. If you've just bought a new car in the UK, this site can cause severe heart palpitations.

Carseekers

www.carseekers.co.uk/

This site offers European sourced cars at European prices. They can even arrange finance for you.

Exclusive Euro Car Imports

www.exclusive-eurocar.co.uk/

Choose from dozens of in-stock cars or use this website to get an online quote.

14. Car Recovery

Automobile Association

www.theaa.co.uk/

Sooner or later it's bound to happen. And usually when you're in a hurry. That gleaming sleek piece of automotive technology that cost an arm and a leg stops working in the middle of nowhere. The AA is the oldest motoring organisation and the website features offers for car insurance, foreign travel insurance, driving lessons and route planning.

Britannia Rescue

www.britanniarescue.com/

Voted Road Rescue 'Best Buy' for 4 years, this site offers membership, route planning and much more.

Green Flag Motoring

www.greenflag.co.uk/

This is the website of one of the UK's largest breakdown / rescue services.

Royal Automobile Club

www.rac.co.uk/

Even if you're not a member, you can still benefit from this site. Of particular note is the superb route finder where you enter the start of your journey and the destination. After a few seconds you'll get a detailed description of your journey which you can print out and take with you.

Vehicle Breakdown

www.vehiclebreakdown.org.uk/

Apart from signing on, there's lots of useful motoring information including preparing your car for the winter.

15. Car Sales

autobytel.co.uk

www.autobytel.co.uk/

The second largest purchase most people make, after a house, is a car. Rather than padding round all the garages, compare the prices on the Internet.

AutoLocate

www.autolocate.co.uk/

Find new and used cars, read car reviews and locate dealers at this well produced website.

AutoTrader Interactive

www.autotrader.co.uk/

The online version of the popular magazine filled with car ads from both dealers and private individuals. Use this site to sell your car privately.

Bristol Street Group

www.bristolstreet.co.uk/

One of the largest dealerships in the UK. Browse the website and find the new or used car you want at the price you want to pay.

The site also details finance, warranty and Bristol Street's after-sales service.

British Car Auctions Group

www.bca-group.com/

To buy a car for the very lowest price, go to an auction. But a warning: the cars are sold 'as seen' so do your homework carefully. Inspect them before bidding and check what price the cars should go for.

Cardata

www.cardata.co.uk/

Claims to match a buyer to a seller every 15 seconds.

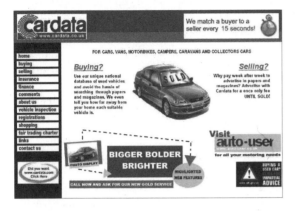

Fish4Cars

www.fish4cars.co.uk/

If you know what you want, search for it on this site. The adverts are from both motor dealers and private individuals. There are thousands of cars advertised and you can add yours online.

Jamjar.com

www.jamjar.com/

Direct Line's car sales branch will help you get a new car for less than many dealers charge.

Parkers Online

www.parkers.co.uk/

Find out what your car is worth, or alternatively, how much you should pay for the car you've got your eye on.

What Car?

www.whatcar.co.uk/

Find the best buys (and the worst) from the website of this famous independent reviewer.

16. Careers

Best People

www.best-people.co.uk/

If you want an IT job, or you're looking for IT staff, visit this site.

CareerZone UK

www.careerzone-uk.com/

The difference between a job and a career, I'm told, is that a career has some sort of progression built in. Here's a place that could help you get the latter.

Fish 4 Jobs

www.fish4jobs.co.uk/

If you're looking for a job, this site has thousands which are conveniently classified.

Head Hunters

www.headhunters.co.uk/

If you're looking for an IT job, this site has lots divided into Contract, Graduate, Permanent and Overseas.

Internet Job Shop

www.internetjobshop.com/

Another opportunity to find a career in IT.

I Resign

www.i-resign.com/

Apart from jobs, this site features a resignation kit which includes sample letters for your boss, financial advice and legal help.

Monster.co.uk

www.monster.co.uk/

Search for a wide range of jobs on this friendly website.

People Bank

www.peoplebank.com/

Prospective employees register their CV with the People Bank and prospective employers search through for suitable candidates.

Workthing

www.workthing.com/

Jobs, advice and training opportunities in Accountancy, Banking, Education, Engineering, Government, Graduate, Human resources, Insurance, IT, Law, Marketing/Sales, Media/Entertainment, Retail, Telecoms and Travel/Leisure.

17. Charities

Amnesty International

www.amnesty.org.uk/

The human race has much to answer for. Amnesty International raises awareness for injustices that we inflict upon each other.

Breast Cancer Campaign

www.bcc-uk.org/cancer/

Visit this website to find out about breast cancer and how to check your breasts, as well as all the latest news about the events and the research.

Cancer Research Campaign

www.crc.org.uk/

One in four people in the UK will suffer from cancer at some time during their life. The Cancer Research Campaign raises money to fund research into treatments and cures.

CharityNet

www.charitynet.org/

This online resource brings together the websites of non-profit making organisations.

Great Ormond Street Hospital

www.gt-ormond-st-hospital.org.uk/

The website of the famous children's hospital detailing its fund-raising activities.

Greenpeace

www.greenpeace.org.uk/

This organisation keeps an eye on our environment and focuses attention on companies and organisations that try to take shortcuts which lead to pollution.

Helping.org

www.helping.org/

The heading on the website says it all: "Helping people make a difference."

Macmillan Cancer Relief

www.macmillan.org.uk/

This UK charity supports people with cancer and their families with specialist information, treatment and care.

Mind

www.mind.org.uk/

The website of the leading mental health charity in England and Wales.

National AIDS Trust

www.nat.org.uk/

Making sure the UK does everything it can in the fight against this dreadful disease.

Prince's Trust

www.princes-trust.org.uk/

The Prince's Trust helps 14–30 year olds to develop confidence, learn new skills and get into work.

Prostate Cancer Charity

www.prostate-cancer.org.uk/

This is the most common male cancer. Visit the site to find out what it is, how to detect it and how it is treated.

18. Chatrooms

A1 Chat Rooms

www.a1chat-rooms.com/

This site offers links to the main chat sites and also lists individual chat sites from around the world. A chatroom is simply a way of talking in real time to someone who could conceivably be anywhere in the world, using the keyboard.

About.com

www.about.com/

This huge resource is divided into subject areas each hosted by a Guide. Log onto the site(s) you're interested in and chat about the subject with the Guide.

Beeb Chat

www.bbc.co.uk/livechat

Auntie has hauled herself into the 21st Century with daily chats, with celebrities frequently joining in. There are details about forthcoming chat sessions with times and topics, and chat transcripts.

Chatrooms Index

www.user.globalnet.co.uk/

This site links to dozens of chatrooms from around the world where you can hold a conversation with whoever happens to be listening.

Dobedo

www.dobedo.co.uk/

Membership is free on this chatroom which enables you to wander around an island with your chosen avatar and talk to others. You can also vote in polls.

Just Chat

www.justchat.co.uk/

You don't need to register with this chat room.

Lycos Chat

lycos-chat.lycos.co.uk/

You choose a handle (an alias) in a choice of rooms based around the theme of a cruise ship.

MSN UK Chat Rooms

chat.msn.co.uk/

Microsoft's chatroom offers chats with celebrities. You can also chat to friends and create your own private chat room.

UKChat

www.ukchat.co.uk/home

You can become a chat host, chat about specific topics or just chat.

Yahoo! Chat

uk.chat.yahoo.com/

Browse around this massive site, wander between the rooms and chat to whoever happens to be there. If you wish, you can select an individual and have a private chat with them.

19. Cinema

BBC Online – Films

www.bbc.co.uk/films

This BBC site features reviews of the latest cinema and video releases, together with interviews and feature articles.

Film Finder

search.yell.com/search/filmsearch

If you're not sure what a particular film is about, this site provides brief summaries of the plots, lists film times and locations. It also features links to fan sites.

Film Unlimited

www.filmunlimited.co.uk/

This Guardian site gives details about the latest films with interviews with the stars.

Odeon

www.odeon.co.uk/

The famous cinema chain is now online. Check out what's on, read about the films and book online.

Scene One

www.sceneone.co.uk/s1/cinema

Find out what's showing at Scene One.

Scoot

cinema.scoot.co.uk/

Enter the name of a town and find out what's on, where and what time. If you're not sure about a film, read the synopses of films currently being shown.

Virgin Net Cinema

www.virgin.net/cinema

Find out about films and where they're being shown; also articles, critics' choices and competitions.

Warner Village Cinemas

www.warnervillage.co.uk/

Find out what's on at your local Warner Cinema, read about the films and book online. Regrettably, the popcorn and drinks must be bought on arrival.

Austin Reed

www.austinreed.co.uk/

Browse through the online branch and then visit a real store to make your purchases. The site features formal and casual clothes for men and women.

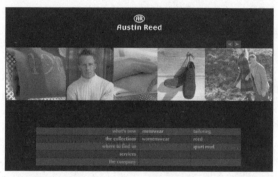

Debenhams

www.debenhams.com/

If you're still not convinced that online clothes shopping is a good idea, you can go virtual window shopping in the online branch of a popular store like Debenhams. This site also includes a list of branches so you can easily buy in the real shop after choosing in the online store.

Dorothy Perkins

www.dorothyperkins.co.uk/

Online shopping has had a mixed press, but contrary to some opinion, it is secure providing you are using a secure connection and you're dealing with a reputable company. Personally I'd rather buy online than drag myself around crowded shops. The disadvantage with buying clothes online is the hassle of having to send them back if they don't fit or simply don't look as good on you as they do on the model.

Freemans

www.freemans.com/

Visit this site and browse through the pages of clothes and shoes for men, women and children.

Gap

www.gap.com/

Not only can you buy this year's collection, you can preview what's coming next season.

Haburi

www.haburi.com/

You can search for clothing items by category or by brand name and then order and pay online.

Kays

www.kaysnet.com/

The website of the famous family clothes catalogue. Browse through the items and buy online.

Marks & Spencer

www.marksandspencer.com/

One of the most famous high street clothing retailers has an online branch where you can browse through the same stock as you would find in the high street.

When you've found what you're looking for, order and pay online using a secure connection.

Next

www.next.co.uk/

The online branch of the trendy high street store originally aimed at those who no longer qualify for Club 18–30 holidays. Now it features clothes for all ages.

Principles

www.principles.co.uk/

Competitions and news of the latest collections are featured with a range of womens' wear which can be searched through by product or style.

Topman

www.topman.co.uk/

Browse through the range of men's clothing and buy online. You can also apply online for a store account.

Yoox

www.yoox.com/

Online retailer offering top designer clothing and accessories.

21. Collecting

Bottle Club

www.thebottleclub.com/

It's amazing what people will collect. This site features bottles, many of which were originally designed to be discarded and re-cycled (as most were) which is why the remainder are so valuable.

Cartophilic Society

www.cardclubs.ndirect.co.uk/

This well-established organization is dedicated to collecting cards. Become a member and enjoy the journal, library and annual card fair.

Coin Collecting

www.buy-coins.co.uk/

This guide to coin collecting features British and foreign coins, including gold, silver, platinum, and those produced by the Royal Mint.

Coincraft

www.coincraft.com/

This site features an excellent glossary of terms and an introduction to coin collecting. Visit the online store to buy or sell British and world coins and banknotes.

CollectiblesNET

www.collectiblesnet.com/

It's in the genes, I'm sure. The human race is an acquisitive species and anything that has more than two or three variants seems to form the basis of a collection. This site covers it all from dolls to stamps, from model soldiers to comics.

Doll Collecting

collectdolls.about.com/

Buy, sell, trade, and discuss everything about dolls, including Barbie and everything related to her.

London Cigarette Card Company

www.londoncigcard.co.uk/

Originally given away with packets of cigarettes so you could have something to read whilst you choked to death. It also includes cards given away with packets of tea.

National Association of Miniature Enthusiasts

www.miniatures.org/

Founded in the early 1970's, this site is not aimed at vertically challenged modellers but for people who make and collect miniatures.

Stanley Gibbons

www.stanleygibbons.com/

Probably the most famous name in the world for stamps. You can bid online, read the history, visit the shop or enter the competitions.

22. Computers

Action Computer Supplies

www.action.com/

Apart from complete computer systems you'll find virtually every computer peripheral you can think of, and several you can't. This well organised site makes it easy to find what you want, which can then be purchased online.

Gateway SpotShop

www.spotshop.co.uk/

You can buy a range of computer hardware, software and networking products from this online store with fast delivery times.

HardwareCentral

www.hardwarecentral.com/

Check out the best hardware products as well as tips and tutorials. You can also subscribe to the free newsletter.

Hewlett-Packard

www.hp.com/

This brilliantly well organised website allows visitors to purchase computer goods online. The site also includes a directory of resellers and help pages.

MISCO Computer Products

www.misco.co.uk/

There are frequently some super deals on hardware, software and peripherals at this online computer store.

PC Direct

www.pcdirect.co.uk/

Before selecting and buying online, check out the reviews and benchmark tests to see if your first choice really is the best deal.

PCHardware.co.uk/

www.pchardware.co.uk/

This site features reviews and comparisons of many of the top brands of computer and computer peripherals.

PC World

www.pcworld.co.uk/

The online branch of the computer superstore has everything on offer that you would be able to buy in the real store. Buy online with a secure connection.

Time Computers

www.timecomputers.com/

The computer store that sells direct to the public is becoming more and more familiar to high street shoppers. The online shop lets you look at the deals on offer and helps you make informed choices.

23. Computer Consumables

Avery Labels

www.avery.com/

Avery produce a huge range of high quality labels for laser and inkjet printers. Many are mounted on an A4 backing sheet and software templates are available to ensure what you print fits exactly onto the label.

InkjetUK

www.inkjetuk.com/

If you do a lot of printing it will be worthwhile opening an account with this computer consumables supplier.

PaperDirect

www.paperdirect.com/

This company produces a wide range of pre-printed matching stationery which you just add text to by printing in the usual way. It's a sort of ready-made corporate image. The products are also available from Vista Papers.

PC-Food

www.pc-food.co.uk/

It was thought that the introduction of the computer would reduce paper wastage. Not so. In fact the reverse is true. Computers actually generate huge quantities of waste paper. This site features everything you need to keep your hungry printer running.

Viking Direct

www.vikingdirect.com/

Viking market a wide range of consumables including pre-printed stationery, labels, printer toner for laser printers, cartridges for inkjet printers and plain white paper in a variety of qualities.

Vista Papers

www.vistapapers.co.uk/

If you're a UK resident, buy your Paper Direct papers from this website.

24. Communications

AT&T Telecommunications

www.att.com/

The AT&T network transports the equivalent of all the books in the Library of Congress every 45 minutes! Find out more interesting facts from the website.

British Telecom

www.bt.com/

This huge site has links for domestic users and business users, and links to education. Also learn about new technologies like the videophone.

Cable & Wireless

www.cw.com/

This global telecommunications company provides a wide range of services to businesses and homes.

Nortel

www.nortelnetworks.com/

Find out about the work and history of this UK company.

NTL

www.ntl.com/

Probably best known in the domestic sector as a cable and interactive TV provider, but there's much more to NTL than that.

Remote Satellite Systems International

www.remotesatellite.com/

Keep abreast of the latest satellite technology, including satellite phones. The site also contains lots of frequently asked questions.

Telewest Communications

www.telewest.co.uk/

Another provider of cable communications to businesses and households. This site give the visitor the chance to learn about the services and job opportunities.

25. Confectionery

Ben & Jerry's Ice Cream

www.benjerry.com/

The trouble with much of the commercial ice-cream is that its manufacture doesn't even include milk, let alone cream. Ice cream dates back to Victorian times when it was made from cream and fruit, and then frozen by placing it in a mould which was turned in ice.

Ben and Jerry's ice cream is much the same, except that the freezing process is a little more in keeping with the 21st Century.

In addition to information about the ice cream, including details of their latest flavour, there are games to be played and some fun activities for the kids.

Cadbury

www.cadbury.co.uk/

Chocolate was first used by the Aztecs, although it was very bitter compared to chocolate bought today. The process by which chocolate is made is a long and fascinating one. Not to mention scientific.

This site gives a vast amount of information about the history of chocolate, where it is grown, the modern manufacturing process and its distribution.

Apart from eating chocolate as a confection, chocolate is also a cooking ingredient and Cadbury have included a recipe section which contains some truly mouth-watering recipes.

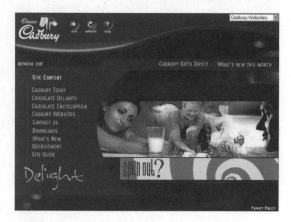

Jelly Belly Online

www.jellybelly.com/

The jelly bean has come a long way since the first products which seemed to taste of nothing but excessive sweetness. Jelly Bellies are made in dozens of flavours that actually taste of what they are supposed to be.

KP Nuts

www.kpnuts.com/

This site is crammed with nutty facts about KP products. There is a new competition each month and a questions and answers page.

Smints

www.smint.com/

Usually found on the counters of filling stations, you get about 40 tiny triangular tabs in a brilliantly designed automatic dispenser. The tabs are rock hard (so don't try chewing them) but are crammed full of flavour. Original Smints and Lemon Smints are common, but look out for Intense Peach. The website also shows flavours not seen in the UK.

Sweet Factory

www.sweet-factory.com/

This is where much of the pick-and-mix candy and confections come from. You can view the products and read the company news.

Walkers Crisps

www.walkers.co.uk/

I restrict the number of packets of crisps in the house as I've found the children start grazing on them. If they're a little bored, they pop off to the pantry and emerge chomping on a bag of crisps. An hour later they don't want any dinner.

This of course is entirely understandable – crisps are very morish.

The Walkers Crisps website gives a fascinating insight into what has become the most popular brand of potato crisp on sale.

26. Consumer Electronics

Comet

www.comet.co.uk/

One of the leading names in consumer electronics. The list of products includes hi-fi, television, video and household products like vacuum cleaners and cookers.

Currys

www.currys.co.uk/

Another popular name that appears less and less on the high street and more and more in retail parks. Search through the products and buy online.

Dixons

www.dixons.co.uk/

This site is one of the best of its type. There's lots of information about all of the products which can usually be found in the stores. Search through this site and choose the product you're interested in. Then, read the reviews and compare specifications with other similar products. When you've decided what you want, buy online using a secure connection.

Powerhouse

www.powerhouse-retail.co.uk/

Formerly the Electricity Board, you'll find washers, dryers, refrigeration, cookers and small domestic appliances, as well as TV and video.

Tempo

www.tempo.co.uk/

This is the online branch of the name usually found in retail parks. This store has the usual mix of household items and computers. Browse though the store and buy online or find your nearest branch.

27. Credit Cards

MasterCard

www.mastercard.com/

Mastercard is one of the two major credit cards and their website provides information about their cards and other services they provide, such as insurance.

Visa

www.visa.com/

A succession of comical TV adverts featuring Dudley Moore, Rowan Atkinson and latterly, Angus Deyton have raised the awareness of the other services offered by this widely recognised credit card.

28. Cruises

P & O Cruises

www.pocruises.com/

If you don't fancy becoming involved in another stampede to claim your piece of beach on the Costa Plenty, why not really get away from it all on a cruise.

29. Device Drivers

Creative

www.europe.creative.com/

The website of the manufacturer of sound cards hosts a library of drivers and utilities. It's worth regularly logging onto driver sites to ensure your computer is always running the latest version.

Driver Forum

www.driverforum.com/

If you're looking for a device driver, this site is worth visiting. You can share device drivers for all manner of hardware products as well as ask about and discuss various drivers.

DriverGuide.com

www.driverguide.com/

If in any doubt about the correct printer driver, visit this comprehensive guide to computer drivers.

Printer Drivers

www.printgrc.com/drivers.cfm

Use this site to find links to the websites of printer manufacturers and download the latest drivers.

ZDNet Updates

updates.zdnet.com/

If you've got an unknown monitor, printer, sound card, scanner, graphics card or modem, search this site for the correct driver.

30. DIY

B&Q

www.diy.com/

Easter Bank Holiday is thought to be the busiest time of the year for stores like B&Q. The weather's usually not good enough to go to the seaside, so it's the time when families begin some improvements which will hopefully be completed before the next Easter Bank Holiday. It's also one of the busiest times for accident and emergency departments with a steady stream of cut fingers and other injuries resulting from monumental bad luck or failure to read the instructions.

The B&Q site offers lots of DIY help and advice as well as online shopping.

Homebase

www.homebase.co.uk/

Once part of Sainsbury's, this home and garden DIY store offers lots of products to make your home more homely. More importantly, it provides lots of ideas to provide inspiration.

Boddington's beer

www.boddingtons.com/

The brewers of the beer dubbed the 'Cream of Manchester' have a particularly light-hearted site providing the user with all manner of snippets about their beer.

One of the highlights of the Cream of Websites is a screensaver which can be downloaded and used on your computer.

Coca Cola

www.coke.com/

This is the best known brand worldwide. Hardly surprising when you see the red and white logo enblazoned across anything and everything. Apart from the removal of one ingredient, the recipe has hardly changed since its launch to US soldiers over half a century ago.

Cocktails

hotwired.lycos.com/cocktail

This site contains recipes for cocktails, and some amusing anecdotes to go with them. The advice here though, is to print out the recipe and mix the drink away from the computer.

Coffee

www.realcoffee.co.uk/

We seem to take so much for granted. A cup of coffee arrives at our desk and we swill it down without a second thought. Yet it's a long way from the bean to the cup. This website offers an insight into the production of coffee and includes a huge number of facts about it. The map shows where most of the world's coffee is grown and gives an explanation of the different types and blends available. There is also an ordering service.

Moet & Chandon

www.moet.com/

Whenever I see a bottle of Moet & Chandon (which actually isn't that often) I'm always reminded of the song by Queen in which the opening line is, 'She drinks Moet & Chandon from a pretty cabinet...'. Why not from a glass? Find out more about the queen of champagnes at this website.

Seven Up

www.7up.com/

I can remember Seven-Up from when I was a boy. I don't believe it's changed much since then. The Seven-Up website contains all the information about the product and who makes it. Also some online games to play. It can take a long time to load this site, but it will be worth it.

Tea

www.clipper-teas.co.uk/

If you like tea, you'll find this site thoroughly enjoyable. You can order tea online as well as finding out about all the different types and blends.

Tia Maria

www.tiamaria.co.uk/

The coffee liqueur's website contains some interesting material – and not just about their drink. If viewing this page you'll need a very good monitor as the print is about the smallest I've ever seen.

Wine

www.winespectator.com/

The best wine you can buy is the one you like, regardless of what the critics may say about it. For lovers of fine wine, the Wine Spectator website is the place to visit.

This site is crammed full of information about fine wines for both the expert and the novice.

32. Education

BBC Education

www.bbc.co.uk/education

This huge resource contains vast amounts of information, much of it based on BBC programmes. Some interactive features are also included.

Education – The British Council

www.britishcouncil.org/education

Find out about teaching courses and qualifications available around the world, and read about student exchanges. The site also includes lots of links to other useful sites.

Education Unlimited

www.educationunlimited.co.uk/

This site is run by the Guardian newspaper and features news and special reports on schools, colleges and higher education.

National Grid for Learning

www.ngfl.gov.uk/

A highly publicised portal for all things educational including teaching, careers, libraries and museums.

National Curriculum

www.nc.uk.net/

Visit this site to see what your children should be learning in their school.

Schoolsnet

www.schoolsnet.com/

Complete directory of schools in the UK. The site also features interactive lessons, forums and education news. There's an online shop where you can buy supplies for the classroom.

Topmarks Education

www.topmarks.co.uk/

This site contains hundreds of categorised links to specialist areas.

33. Estate Agents

Estate Agents

www.estateagents.tv/

Sellers and buyers can search a directory of house-moving-related services including removal companies, gardeners and electricians.

Halifax Property

www.halifaxproperty.co.uk/

Apart from providing mortgages, this site also provides help and advice for those who want to buy or sell houses, flats and apartments.

National Association of Estate Agents

www.naea.co.uk/

This is the trade association for the UK property industry, with information about membership, buying and selling property, and property listings.

PropertyLive

www.propertylive.co.uk/

This database lists thousands of houses and flats for sale or rent, with a handy estate agent finder.

UK Property Register

www.property-realestate-uk.com/

They say the three important points to consider when choosing a property are location, location and location. Get information about the places and search the database of commercial property for sale or for lease.

Territorium

www.teramedia.co.uk/

Buying a house is not like buying anything else. The process is endless and expensive. This company aims to make the conveyancing process much faster for all concerned. Buyers and vendors can monitor their property transaction online.

34. Ethnic

Black Britain

www.blackbritain.co.uk/

This is a site especially for Black African Caribbean people contains news, shopping, features and jobs. There's also the opportunity of online discussion.

Chronicle World

www.chronicleworld.org/

Modern London owes a great deal to the work of black immigrants. But their input goes back much further. This site looks at their contributions since AD 50.

Multi-Ethnic Britain

www.blink.org.uk/

There's a great deal of interesting and informative material on this site together with facts and figures and lots of useful links to follow.

Windrush – BBC Education

www.bbc.co.uk/education/windrush

A tribute to the arrival of the first Caribbean immigrants in 1948 on board the Windrush.

35. Fashion

Fashion UK

www.widemedia.com/fashionuk

A directory of designers, models, and labels is the main feature of this site.

femail.co.uk

www.femail.co.uk/

What's 'in' today is frequently 'out' tomorrow. But don't throw it away. They say what goes around, comes around and before long it will be the height of fashion once again.

London College of Fashion

www.lcf.linst.ac.uk/

If you fancy a career in fashion, visit this website. You can find out what you'll need to get in and what you'll do if you get there.

Lucire

lucire.com/

The online fashion magazine features everything that's in fashion.

Museum of Costume

www.museumofcostume.co.uk/

The virtual site of the Bath museum which features all the important landmarks in this fickle industry.

Vogue

www.vogue.co.uk/

Apart from beauty advice and tips, you'll get to see the latest from the catwalks.

36. Ferries

Ferrybooker

www.ferrybooker.com/

Provides a ferry/channel crossing guide with timetables for passenger service providers.

Ferry View

www.seaview.co.uk/

It's worth spending time reading through this site before deciding which ferry company to choose.

Stena Line

www.stenaline.co.uk/

Stena Line runs a passenger ferry between GB, Northern Ireland, Republic of Ireland, and Holland. Information includes fares, times and boat details.

SeaFrance Ferries

www.seafrance.co.uk/

If you're considering crossing the Channel by water then this website is worth visiting as it details booking information, fares, times and special offers.

P&O Ferries

www.poferries.com/home/routes.htm

This service runs from several UK ports to numerous European ports. All the information about sailings, routes and times is instantly available here. It's far quicker than using the telephone.

37. Flight booking

a2bAirports.com

www.a2bairports.com/

You can book a flight online and also check out the weather at your destination.

Airline Network

www.airnet.co.uk/

You can view flight times and book online at this well organised website.

EasyJet

www.easyjet.com/

Once you've chosen your destination you can choose a flight either by price (in which case you may have to compromise on the date) or by date (in which case you may have to compromise on price). You can then book online with this 'no-frills' airline which doesn't even issue a ticket.

Expedia UK

expedia.msn.co.uk/

This MSN site seems to have everything covered. You can get flight information, hotel information or hire car prices. There is even a currency calculator.

travelstore.com

www.travelstore.com/

Another 'do everything' site featuring flight and hotel booking, car rental and travel insurance. The site includes currency information and the obligatory weather reports.

38. Flowers

0800-Blossoms.com

www.0800-blossoms.com/

It's amazing what people will call themselves just to be first on the list. But this company does send out some beautiful blooms worldwide.

Flowers Directory

www.flowersdirect.co.uk/

Promises next-day delivery of floral bouquets and arrangements. You can even get email reminders of dates on which flowers should be sent.

Interflora

www.interflora.co.uk/

Probably the most famous name in flower delivery. You can view the bouquets and get them delivered to almost anywhere in the world.

Marks & Spencer

www.marksandspencer.com/

Buy a bouquet online here. The flowers are fresh and last a surprisingly long time.

Simply Flowers

www.simplyflowers.co.uk/

This superb site includes pictures of the bouquets currently available for ordering.

Teleflorist

www.teleflorist.co.uk/

After choosing an appropriate bunch of blooms, you can order using the secure ordering facility and get it delivered almost anywhere in the world.

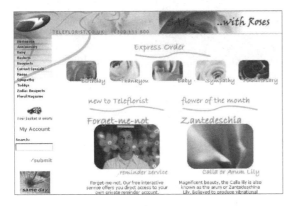

39. Food

British Nutrition Foundation

www.nutrition.org.uk/

Get the nutritional facts and figures and find out about events, news, publications and educational programs.

Creative Kitchen

www.creative-kitchen.co.uk/

This hot site (forgive the pun) includes cooking tips and some really simple recipes. Unlike many opening animated introductions, it's worth watching this one.

DEFRA – Food and Drink

www.defra.gov.uk/

This site, brought to you by the Department for the Environment, Food & Rural Affairs, provides sound guidance for a range of foods including meat and eggs.

European Food Information Council

www.eufic.org/

Search for a food and get scientific, safety and nutritional information.

Food – BBC Online

www.bbc.co.uk/food/

Mainly to support the BBC TV programme, this site features a huge collection of recipes from the TV programme and BBC radio programmes.

Taste

www.taste.co.uk/

Carlton TV's answer to the BBC site features a range of recipes and information about foods.

40. Furniture

FurnitureFind.com

www.furniturefind.com/

Find the items you want for your living room, dining room, and bedroom. Items include reclining chairs, sofas, desks and chairs.

Furniture, Interiors and Gardens

www.fig.co.uk/

This online furniture directory features the work of interior designers as well as companies.

Furniture-on-line

www.furniture-on-line.co.uk/

Rather than trekking round high street furniture shops, browse through the range in this online showroom of modern and traditional styles.

Habitat

www.habitat.net/

Originally Terence Conran's brainchild, Habitat specialises in trendy furniture and fittings for trendy people.

IKEA

www.ikea.co.uk/

This Scandinavian furniture company is big on style yet low on price. Get assembly tips, view furniture in actual rooms and locate your nearest IKEA store.

Interior Internet

www.interiorinternet.com/

After browsing through the wide range of products, you can locate your nearest retailer.

Magnet

www.magnet.co.uk/

View the range of fitted bedrooms, bathrooms and kitchens.

MFI Homeworks

www.mfi.co.uk/

Frank Mullard started Mullard Furniture Industries in a railway station kiosk. MFI have come a long way since then, shaking off their trashy image and producing some really well-designed products that you assemble at home.

41. Gadgets

Gadget & Gizmos

www.gizmos-uk.com/

There's lots of things you'd like, several things you want, but nothing you actually need in this online gadget shop. You can get updates by email to ensure you're really abreast of the latest gizmos.

Gadget City

www.gadgetcity.co.uk/

The site includes extreme sports equipment, and lots of hi-tech gadgetry.

Gadget Shop

www.thegadgetshop.co.uk/

A great selection of gift ideas for the man or woman who has everything. Buy online using the secure connection.

Gadgets UK

www.gadgetsuk.com/

A veritable feast of goodies and gadgets including lava lamps, key rings, lights and lasers. Browse through the stock and buy online using a secure connection.

Innovations

www.innovations.co.uk/

This site sells an assortment of gadgets. If it's got a battery in it, it's probably here.

I Want One of Those

www.iwantoneofthose.com/

More stuff you don't need but would really like. Use the search facility to seek out the gifts you want for others, but mostly for the gifts you'd like for yourself.

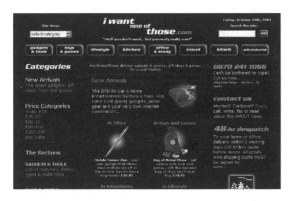

UKool.com

www.ukool.com/

Loads of hi-tech gadgets with detailed descriptions on sale at this online store.

42. Gambling

Casino On Net

www.casinoonnet.co.uk/

The roll of the dice, the spin of the wheel, the thrill of the bet, the empty feeling in your pocket... It's just like visiting a real casino.

Flutter.com

www.flutter.com/

Rather than betting against a bookie, you can declare your own odds and bet against other punters.

GamCare

www.gamcare.org.uk/

For some, gambling is a drug. If you need help to get you off the drug, visit this website.

Gold Strike Hotel & Gambling Hall

www.goldstrike-jean.com/

This online casino is based on a hotel in a mythical town called Jean.

Jamba

www.jamba.co.uk/

A variety of casino type games, plus others like Bingo are available at this online casino.

Ladbrokes Casino

www.ladbrokescasino.com/

Once you've downloaded the free software you can play online games such as blackjack, poker, roulette, craps, baccarat and keno.

Premier Info

www.premier-info.com/

Mug up on the form before betting.

Sportingbet

www.sportingbet.com/

You can bet on most major sporting events in any currency you choose.

Dreamcast Europe

www.dreamcast-europe.com/

This is the official Sega site which outlines the company's products including the latest games for the Sega Dreamcast games console.

Flipside

uk.flipside.com/

This online playground includes a variety of puzzles, card games, arcade games and casino simulations. If you register on this site you can play for points.

Games Workshop

www.games-workshop.com/

Futuristic war-gaming is probably the easiest way to describe the subject of this site.

Games Domain

www.gamesdomain.co.uk/

If you get stuck with one of the games, visit this site to find the cheat to get you out of trouble.

GameSpot UK

www.gamespot.co.uk/

You can download a variety of PC games and get help if you get stuck trying to play it.

PC Zone

www.pczone.co.uk/

Apart from the hints, tips and cheats, there's lots of downloads and news and reviews of the latest games. If you get stuck, visit the forum to get the answers.

Nintendo: Game Boy

www.nintendo.com/

If playing arcade games on the move is more appropriate, visit this Nintendo site for all your Gameboy needs, including information about new games and features.

Shockwave

www.shockwave.com/

You can play a range of classic games online using the Shockwave software freely downloadable from this site.

44. Garden

BBC Gardeners' World

www.gardenersworld.beeb.com/

Especially for those who have green fingers and muddy knees, this site features hints and tips to make the most of your plot.

e-garden.co.uk/

www.e-garden.co.uk/

Visit this site for all your gardening needs including gifts for the gardener.

Gardening365

www.oxalis.co.uk/

Visit this site regularly to get seasonal tips and advice about planting, watering, feeding, insects and just about everything else.

GardenWorld

www.gardenworld.co.uk/

This site lists dozens of garden centres around the UK.

Large Scale On-Line

www.largescaleonline.com/

If you feel your garden needs something of interest that doesn't need pruning or cropping, why not install a large scale garden railway running on steam or electric? This site offers lots of tips about building a railway including where to buy the track and how to lay it. Lots of pictures for motivation.

National Gardens Scheme

www.ngs.org.uk/

If you've got a nice garden (with or without the railway), why not open it to the public and make money for charity? Here, find out how to do it or use the locator to pinpoint a nearby scheme member.

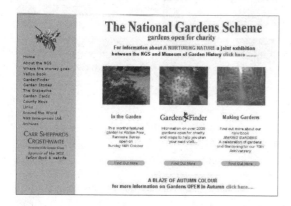

Plants Magazine

www.plants-magazine.com/

This is the online version of the popular magazine featuring gardening hints and tips and back issues.

45. Genealogy

English Record Offices and Archives

www.oz.net/~markhow/englishros.htm

A comprehensive listing of UK archives by county is invaluable for those trying to trace their roots.

Genealogy.com

www.genealogy.com/

The website of one of the leading genealogy software developers. It includes articles, records and help.

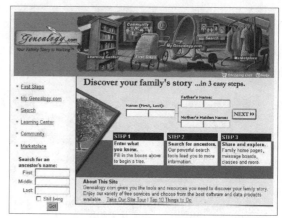

GENUKI

www.genuki.org.uk/

This site provides a comprehensive guide to researching UK and Ireland from overseas, and includes links to documents and genealogical societies.

Public Record Office

www.pro.gov.uk/

Probably the first place to visit if you're trying to plot your family history. The site includes lots of help and links to other sites.

Society of Genealogists

www.sog.org.uk/

This London organization claims to have the largest collection of parish records in the British Isles.

UK Genealogy Resources

genealogy.8k.com/

The 'How to Research' section provides valuable pointers for people embarking on genealogical research.

UK Genealogy USA

www.ukgenealogyusa.free-online.co.uk/

Visit this site to get help plotting your family tree or finding lost relatives.

46. Gifts

Alternative Gift Company

www.alt-gifts.com/

You can search this site for unusual gifts for men, women, children and the home.

Find-me-a-gift.com

www.find-me-a-gift.com/

A huge range of presents for all occasions is featured on this website.

Gift Delivery Company

www.giftdeliveryco.com/

One of the strengths of this site is the gift finder which should be able to give you some ideas.

Alternatively you can choose a gift from one of the categories which includes corporate gifts to give the workers a pat on the back.

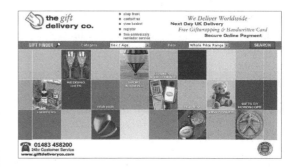

Gift Fair

www.gift-fair.co.uk/

Toys, stationery and books are amongst the hundreds of gifts available for online order and fast delivery.

Gift Ideas

www.gotogifts.co.uk/

If you're looking for humorous or unusual gifts, this website gives plenty of choice.

Gift Time

www.gifttime.co.uk/

This site offers a wide range of gifts for Christmas, birthdays and Valentine's Day with secure online ordering.

Gifts.com

www.gifts.com/

This Reader's Digest site divides gifts into categories including Him, Her, Home, Indoors, Outdoors, Travel, Kids and Techtrends. You can search for a specific gift or get ideas for gifts. When you've chosen, buy online.

Presents Direct

www.presentsdirect.com/

This site offers a good range of useful and not-so-useful presents for all occasions and tastes. There is next day delivery on most items which can be dispatched worldwide.

47. Government

British Monarchy

www.royal.gov.uk/

This is the official site of the UK Monarchy and is crammed with information about the royal family.

Cabinet Office

www.cabinet-office.gov.uk/

An excellent site for anyone wanting to find out more about the workings of the UK's decision makers.

No. 10 Downing Street

www.number-10.gov.uk/

This is the official site the house behind the most famous door in the world, occupied by the British Prime Minister. There's also a virtual tour of the building.

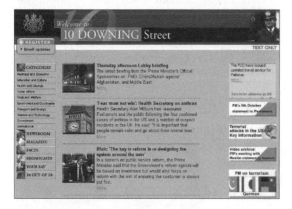

Conservatives

www.conservatives.org.uk/

If you're not sure what the policies are, visit this site to find out, and to get information about the key figures that make up this UK political party.

Houses of Parliament

www.parliament.uk/

Everything about the centre of the oldest democracy in the world is crammed into this site.

Labour Party

www.labour.org.uk/

If you're not sure what the policies are, visit this site to find out, and to get information about the key figures that make up this UK political party.

Liberal Democrats

www.libdems.org.uk/

If you're not sure what the policies are, visit this site to find out, and to get information about the key figures that make up this UK political party.

parliamentlive.tv

www.parliamentlive.tv/

If you can't get Parliament broadcasts on your TV, visit this site which broadcasts over the web. (Don't set your watch by the chimes of Big Ben as there can be a delay of as much as a minute.)

White House, The

www.whitehouse.gov/

The official site of the seat of US government which includes news and policies.

48. Health

Handbag.com

www.handbag.com/health

Get hints and tips on female health and beauty from the site aimed at women.

Healthworks

www.healthworks.co.uk/

Visit this site to get daily health tips to keep you in tip top condition.

Health In Focus

www.healthinfocus.co.uk/

A collection of chat, newsletters and polls with lots of information on illnesses, treatments and symptoms.

iCircle

www.icircle.com/

This women's site features a health section covering most female issues including breast cancer, fertility, pregnancy, sexual health and nutrition.

Men's Health

www.menshealth.com/

This is the website of the popular men's magazine and includes articles on fitness, weight and sex. There's also a daily survey and tips for a healthier life.

NetDoctor

www.netdoctor.co.uk/

I'm not sure that providing a layman with medical information is really a good idea but if you do want to use this site to find out what you think is wrong with you, follow it up with a visit to your GP.

Surgery Door

www.surgerydoor.co.uk/

This site covers a range of alternative medicines as well as conventional therapies. There's a useful first aid section and conditions are listed alphabetically.

Wellbeing

www.wellbeing.com/

A joint venture by Boots and Granada which provides lots of advice and news. There's also a range of healthcare products offered for sale.

49. Hobbies

British Origami Society

www.britishorigami.org.uk/

It's amazing what you can make by taking a piece of paper and folding it. Visit this site and get instructions to fold some amazing models.

British Surfing Association, The

britsurf.co.uk/

Take a plank of wood and a wave and you're off. Well, almost. Find out all about where to surf, what to wear and what to stand on. Oh yes, and there's a serious alternative to a VW combi van as your preferred means of transport...

Centerline Hobbies

www.centerlinehobbies.com/

Lots of classified adverts about all manner of hobbies.

Fishing.co.uk

www.fishing.co.uk/

I've never been able to see the point in sitting by a river bank in the freezing cold teaching a worm to swim on the end of a line, but fishing is one of the most popular hobbies in the UK.

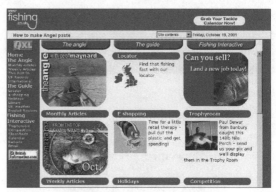

Kite Shop, The

www.kiteshop.co.uk/

This online store contains everything you need to get involved in kite making and flying.

Monarch Knitting & Quilts

www.monarchknitting.com/

This takes me back. Endless nights listening to the clickety-click of mum's knitting needles. But what superb pullovers she made. This site offers lots of help and advice for knitters.

ScubaDuba

www.scubaduba.com/

The website of Self Contained Underwater Breathing Apparatus followers. Visit this site to find out all about how to become a frogman.

Worldwide Woodwork

www.worldwide-woodwork.co.uk/

This is a complete course based on British carpentry and joinery techniques. Classes are available for all levels.

50. Holidays

Airtours

www.airtours.co.uk/

Visit this website and book a complete holiday package.

Ebookers.com

www.ebookers.com/

You can get a range of discounted flights, hotels and car hire.

Expedia UK

expedia.msn.co.uk/

This superb site has lots of bargain holidays.

First Resort

www.thefirstresort.com/

You can search for a holiday by price, destination, date and duration.

Lastminute.com

www.lastminute.com/

This company specialises in late booking for flights, holidays, car hire and hotel accommodation. If you can stand the tension of waiting to the last minute to book, then you can get some great deals.

Trailfinders

www.trailfinder.com/

If you don't want an army-style regimented holiday but want to please yourself, visit this site and put together your own itinerary which could include flights, tours, hotels, and car hire.

Travelocity

www.travelocity.co.uk/

If you want a one-stop holiday solution, including getting there and back, this could be the place.

travelstore.com

www.travelstore.com/

Insurance and currency conversion are key elements of this site which sells everything for your holiday.

51. Home Security

Alert Electrical

www.alertelectrical.com/

This company supplies a wide range of burglar alarm kits, CCTV, cameras and security lighting. There are frequently special offers and you can buy online.

Bridgewood Home Security Systems

www.bridgewood-home-security.co.uk/

I'm not convinced a burglar alarm that simply rings a siren outside the house is any use whatsoever. Whenever a house alarm is sounding, nobody seems to take any notice and merely assumes it's a false alarm. In fact, the best time to rob a house seems to be when the alarm is ringing. Bridgewood offers monitored home security systems combining fire and burglar alarms which means that somebody is monitoring the system and the police are called if the alarm is triggered.

Euro Security

www.euroalarms.co.uk/

This company can supply and fit security systems including CCTV systems.

Falcon Security

www.falcon-security.com/

This company supplies a wide range of security products for the home.

Home Office – Crime Prevention Advice

www.homeoffice.gov.uk/crimprev/cp_index.htm

This site offers lots of useful advice to help you protect your property and some help should you fall victim to crime.

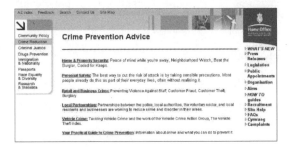

Intellihome

www.intellihome.be/

This company supplies products to automate your home including computer controlled lighting.

Neighbourhood Watch

www.nwatch.org.uk/

Makes neighbours aware of their surroundings, with scheme information and practical advice.

Planet CCTV

www.planetcctv.com/trgrsp.html

This company can supply a range of CCTV with video recording and web-based surveillance systems.

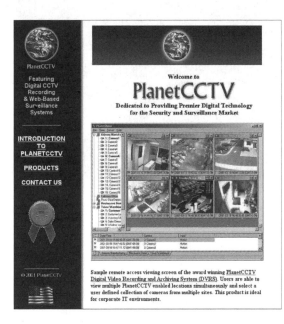

52. Hotels

A–to–Z Hotel Finder

www.from-a-z.com/

Access to over 15,000 UK hotels/reduced rates.

British Hotel Reservation Centre

www.bhrc.co.uk/

Search this London-based reservation company's database of thousands of hotels, B&Bs and apartments. With maps, photos and descriptions.

Country House Hotels of Britain

www.country-house-hotels.com/

This site features a 'clickable' map to locate hotels, B&Bs and other lodgings in the UK.

Expotel Hotel Reservations

www.expotel.co.uk/

Use this website to get discount rates for hotel accommodation in the UK and Ireland.

Hotel Shop

www.thehotelshop.com/

If you want something a little less than the absolute best, visit this site for accommodation on a budget, and book online.

THG – The Hotel Guide

www.hotelguide.com/

This site features a massive database of over 60,000 hotels around the world. Search by a range of criteria.

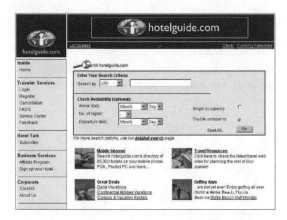

UK Best Hotel and Inn Directory

www.best-hotel.co.uk/

This site offers some of the best accommodation in the UK.

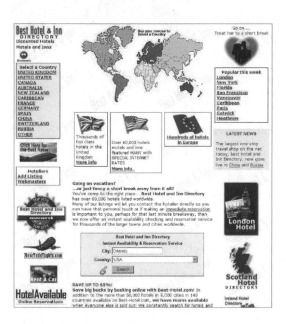

VirtualHotels.com

www.virtualhotels.com/

Look at photos and read the descriptions of over 13,000 hotels in the UK.

53. In-Car Entertainment

Alpine Europe

www.alpine-europe.com/

The website of one of the top names in In-Car Entertainment. Visit this site and see all the latest ear-bashing gadgets for the dashboard.

Autoleads

www.autoleads.co.uk/

Having got a really nice in car hi-fi you will want to install it properly and this site will be able to provide you with details about all the fittings and fixings you'll need.

Blaupunkt UK

www.blaupunkt.co.uk/

Blaupunkt produces a wide range of In-Car Entertainment equipment including amplifiers and large speakers ensuring that pedestrians will be able to hear the music before they hear the engine.

Car Audio Discount

www.caraudiodiscount.com/

This company supplies a wide range of ICE with comparisons and installation tips for experts and novices.

Car Hi-Fi Centre

www.car-hi-fi-centre.co.uk/

You can find lots of special offers on ICE products from this company.

Drive Time

www.drive-time.co.uk/

Apart from a huge range of In-car Entertainment there are plenty of satellite navigation systems available for retro fitting to your car. If you don't fancy cutting holes in the car, let this company do it for you.

Motorspeed

www.motorspeed.co.uk/

Offers a wide range of motor accessories including In-Car Entertainment packages.

MCS Direct

www.mcs-direct.co.uk/

There's a wide range of ear-bashing sound systems which you can buy online via a secure connection.

54. Insurance

Admiral Insurance Services

www.admiral-insurance.co.uk/

One of the top names in car insurance in the UK.

CGNU UK

www.cgnugroup.com/

This large insurance group was formed as a result of the merger of Commercial Union and General Accident.

Churchill Insurance

www.churchill.co.uk/

Heavily advertised company offering travel, motor, home and pet insurance.

Direct Line

www.directline.com/

Fill out an online form, get a quote and buy insurance online for vehicles, the home, pets, travel, and life.

insure.co.uk

www.insure.co.uk/

This site offers quotations for car, household and travel insurance online. If you like the quote you can buy online and also use the site to make a claim.

Moneyextra – Insurance

www.moneyextra.com/insurance/

You can receive insurance quotes and buy online for motor, home, travel and contents insurance.

Screentrade

www.screentrade.com/

Compare quotes from leading insurance companies and buy car insurance online. You can also make insurance claims online.

UK Insurance Web Guide

www.uk-insurance-web.co.uk/

This site is a directory of insurance brokers and companies. You can get quotes for home, travel, car and life cover, and help with insurance jargon.

AllSearchEngines

www.allsearchengines.co.uk/

This search engine allows users to search by keyword or using a directory. You can also get a free email account at this site.

LyricFind.com

www.lyricfind.com/

Enter the song title, artist and album to search this massive database for the lyrics.

NetNames

msn.netnames.net/

If you want to check if a particular domain name has been registered, enter the name into the box provided to search for it. If it isn't in use, find out how to register it for your own use.

Postcodes & Zipcodes

www.copywriter.co.uk/resource/

Choose *Postcode lookup* from the list on the left to find a the whereabouts of postcode or zipcode.

Royal Mail Postcodes

www.royalmail.co.uk/paf/

You can search for a postcode from an address or an address from a postcode on this superb site. Other features include tracking a parcel.

Scoot People Finder

people.scoot.co.uk/

Use this popular search facility to find people by surname, (with or without initials/forenames), town or postcode.

Directory Enquiries

www.192.com/

You'll need to register first and then you'll have 20 free searches per month. Enter the name of a person and the location and find their phone number (as long as they're not ex-directory).

Yellow Pages

www.yell.com/

www.yell.co.uk/

The online version of the famous directory is far easier to use than any book-based directory and provides far more information, including a map to show you how to get there. Simply type in a name and/or a job description and a location for a list of matches.

56. Internet Service Providers

AOL

www.aol.com

America On Line is probably one of the most famous providers due to huge amounts of advertising both on TV and in the press. They also give away huge quantities of CD ROMs containing their software and free Internet time.

AT&T Broadband

www.attbroadband.com/

This is one of the largest providers of broadband services. Visit this site to view the pricing.

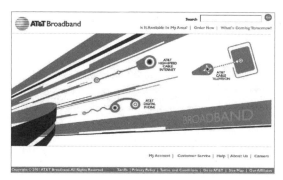

Claranet

www.clara.net/

This company seems to offer just about every variation including unmetered and leased lines for home and business.

Con X

www.conx.co.uk/

Subscribe to this ISP and get free connection.

Freedom2Surf

www.mite.net/

The term 'free' relates to the freedom you get with broadband connection, anytime services and leased lines.

Guide to UK Free ISPs

www.ukfreeisps.abelgratis.co.uk/

This up-to-date directory details free ISPs and provides details including the cost of telephone support.

MSN

www.msn.com/

The Microsoft Network offers a range of dial up and broadband connections.

Tiscali

www.tiscali.co.uk/

Another ISP offering free Internet access, multiple emails and webspace.

57. Internet Shopping

About Online Shopping

onlineshopping.about.com/

There's lots of help and advice for the online shopper on this About.com site.

Ciao!

www.uk.ciao.com/

Use this site to submit positive and negative comments about online stores. You can, of course, also read what others have said.

Goldfish Guide

www.goldfishguide.com/

There's lots of shopping help and advice available at this site. It also contains a number of links to approved outlets.

LetsBuyIt.com

www.letsbuyit.com/

This is co-buying at its very best. Items are offered for sale at a given price. You agree to buy at that price, but if more people buy, the price comes down.

MSN Shopping

shopping.msn.co.uk/

A virtual high street with links to lots of shops covering just about everything you could possibly want to buy.

Office of Fair Trading

www.oft.gov.uk/html/shopping/

Just as in the real world, not every virtual trader is as honest as you might expect. This site offers lots of advice about spotting the rogues and what to do it you get caught up in a scam.

ShopSpy

www.shopspy.co.uk/

Prospective online shoppers should visit this site before buying to see how various traders are performing.

Which? – Shopping

www.which.net/shopping/contents.html

Apart from legal advice you can make purchases from this site's approved retail partners.

58. Investments

E*Trade UK

www.etrade.co.uk/

You can do your research for free and get up-to-the-minute prices and financial news.

Ft.com

www.ft.com/

This is the Financial Times online and provides financial news from around the world.

FTSE International

www.ftse.com/

Visit this site to get the latest footsie figures and the latest financial news.

Interactive Investor

www.iii.co.uk/

If you fancy your chances share dealing then log onto this site and get all the information first, including stock prices and some invaluable tips.

London Stock Exchange

www.londonstockexchange.com/

More information about buying and selling from the official site of London's famous stock exchange.

Nasdaq UK

www.nasdaq-uk.com/

The Nasdaq site features share prices for British and US stocks, market news and a guide to investing in US stocks.

Stockmarket

www.moneyworld.co.uk/stocks/

This site includes a daily business report as well as current exchange rates.

Teleshare

www.teleshare.co.uk/

Visit this site to get access to real-time share prices.

59. Kids

Argosphere

www.argosphere.net/

Argosphere offers a really well produced and safe site which kids (and adults) will enjoy strolling around. There are a variety of interactive tasks and exercises which can be either worked on online, or downloaded and used offline. The topics are diverse and sometimes slightly off-beat.

BBC Education

www/bbc.co.uk/education/home

The Beeb's education site is always worth a visit. There's lots of material for children of all ages.

BritKid

www.britkid.org/

This site is quite unlike any other. It's intended to make kids think about the world around them. It confronts racism and racial issues in a way in which they can understand. There are situations to resolve and descriptions to get you thinking.

This site is well worth visiting, and not just by children.

Gurlpages

www.gurlpages.com/

This superb site has lots of interesting and useful bits and pieces for the fairer sex.

Kids World 2000

now2000.com/bigkidnetwork/zoos.html

Visit this site for dozens of links to the home pages of zoos and aquariums, mainly in the United States but also elsewhere.

Sesame Street

www.sesameworkshop.org/

The online spin-off from the ground-breaking TV series. Lots of activities and lots of fun is only part of the attraction.

Star Tower

www.mape.org.uk/startower/

For me, one of the highlights from this continuously developing site is the control activity featuring Unit the robot. You may choose from two activities (Apple Picking and Balloon Bursting) which involve providing Unit with instructions to control its position as well as Unit's head which can be raised and lowered. This is an excellent introduction to the principles of control.

Yahooligan

www.yahooligans.com/

The Yahooligan site is a safe area for kids with lots of jokes and fun activities, but also thought-provoking comment.

Yuckiest

www.yucky.com/

The yuckiest site on the web is accurately named. One of the popular areas is *Your Yucky Body* which explains why we burp, why poo is brown and what we find in our ears!

60. Leisure

David Lloyd Leisure

www.davidlloydleisure.co.uk/

Press-ups, lifting weights and working up a sweat is not my idea of relaxation, but if it's yours, this website will be worth a visit as it outlines the facilities and directs you to the nearest centre.

Frontier Leisure

www.frontier-leisure.co.uk/

Living under canvas is also not my first choice for a leisure pursuit, but if it's yours, this company sells everything you need to get closer to nature.

PSW Leisure

www.psw-leisure.co.uk/

Visit this site to find out how to hire simulators, bouncy castles and ejector seats. Again, being rocketed into the air is not really how I like to relax, but there are other attractions for hire for school fairs and corporate entertainment.

Tickets-Direct

www.apollo-leisure.co.uk/

Book tickets online from here.

61. Lifestyle

Absolute Match

www.absolutematch.com/

Whether you're looking for a lasting relationship or a date at the local picture house, Absolute Match should be able to find your ideal partner.

GaytoZ

www.gaytoz.com/

This site is a directory linking to over 5,000 services for gay people.

Gemini

www.eclipse.co.uk/benson/dating/

Get your perfect heterosexual or homosexual partner for a lasting relationship or something shorter.

Lifestyle.co.uk

www.lifestyle.co.uk/

This directory points you to all manner of sites to improve your lifestyle.

Low-Fat Lifestyle Forum

www.mardiweb.com/lowfat/

Helps you prepare low-fat meals. Recipes include vegetarian, starters, breakfast and meat dishes.

QX Magazine

www.qxmag.co.uk/

An online resource for gays and lesbians featuring news about clubs, film reviews and events.

62. Loans

24 Hour Loans

www.24hour-loans.co.uk

You can apply online for a secured personal loan for home improvements, a new car or a holiday. This company also offer a debt consolidation service to enable you to clear all outstanding finance and make it into one single repayment.

About Loans

www.about-loans.co.uk/

If you're not sure which loan to choose, visit this site which compares all types of loan offered by various companies. There's also a loan calculator to help you work out what the repayments would/should be.

Capital Investors

www.finance-loans-money.com/

You can apply for any type of loan for any purpose, including clearing existing loans.

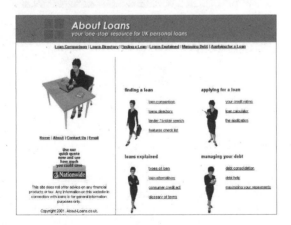

Easy-Loans

www.easy-loans.co.uk/

This site offers loans for home owners for most purposes.

Loan...loan...loans!

www.loan-loan-loans.co.uk/

The name gives it away – it's a loan company.

Money Extra

www.moneyworld.co.uk/rates/

This well laid out site provides valuable advice for those considering borrowing money.

This is Money

www.thisismoney.com/howto.html

More advice on credit cards and other loans.

Your Loan

www.your-loan.co.uk/

This company specialises in debt consolidation to enable you to clear all of your debts and get just one single payment. You need to be a home owner and you can apply online.

63. Magazines

Bike Net Magazine

www.bikenet-magazine.com/

All the latest road and race news and views from the world of two wheels.

Bizarre Magazine

www.bizarremag.com/

This aptly titled magazine provides an alternative slant to science and technology.

British Magazines Direct

www.britishmagazines.com/

You can subscribe online to any of over 3,500 UK publications.

Cosmopolitan

www.cosmomag.com/

The online version of the popular fashion magazine for the thinking reader.

Fast Car

www.fastcar.co.uk/

Not a shopping trolley in sight, this is pure power and speed.

GQ

www.gq-magazine.co.uk/

One of the few men's magazines that isn't crammed with pictures of women.

Hello!

www.hello-magazine.co.uk/

Lots of light reading with interviews with celebrities and politicians as well as cooking tips.

Maxim

www.maxim-magazine.co.uk/

The online version of the men's magazine featuring hard hitting comment, feature articles and light-hearted banter.

Rolling Stone Magazine

www.rollingstone.com/

One of the oldest pop magazines is now online with news, views and interviews.

Smash Hits

www.smashhits.net/

Pop gossip, interviews and previews.

Q Magazine

www.q4music.com/

Another music and entertainment magazine online.

Time Out

www.timeout.com/

Simply add the name of a capital city after the address to get local news.

Uploaded

www.uploaded.com/

A lad's magazine written in laddish style covering anything and everything lads are interested in.

Wallpaper

www.wallpaper.com/

A website befitting a magazine advocating style, class and taste.

64. Maps and Mapping

EasyMap

www.easymap.co.uk/

Enter the name of a street and get a detailed zoomable map pinpointing the exact location.

Garmin

www.garmin.com/

Garmin manufactures receivers which collect and process data from the constellation of satellites put into orbit by the USA. Although originally for military purposes, the Global Positioning System (GPS) is now available to the general public enabling anyone to pinpoint their location very accurately.

Getmapping.com

www.getmapping.com/

Enter a postcode and get a birds-eye view of the area which you can then buy.

Global Positioning Systems

www.globalpositioningsystems.co.uk/

Buy GPS receivers from this online store.

Maps Worldwide

www.mapsworldwide.co.uk/

Whether it's for cycling or bird watching, this site will be able to provide a map to get you there. And back.

Street Finder

www.streetmap.co.uk/

www.streetmap.com/

Enter a postcode or grid reference and a detailed map of the area will be drawn with the exact place marked at the centre. You can zoom in and out of the map to get just the right amount of detail.

There are plain maps and those showing the fare zones.

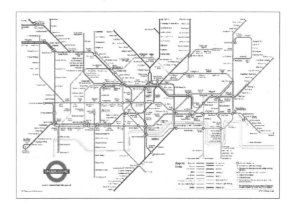

VDO Dayton

www.vdodayton.com/

The website of the manufacturer of high quality satellite navigation systems for cars.

Tiger Mapping Service

tiger.census.gov/

High quality US maps and other geographical resources.

Tube map

www.thetube.com/

Find your way around the oldest and most extensive underground railway system by bringing the map of the London Underground into your computer.

65. Miscellaneous

Build a Car

www.kit-cars.com/

Anyone can walk into a showroom and buy a car – assuming you have the money. But if you've got a modicum of skill, you can build your own. The problem with kit cars is that many of them have been put on the road before they've been properly completed. As a result they look like, well, kit cars. A well built, well finished kit car can be every bit as good as a factory built car – some would say better.

This site lists most of the major kit manufacturers and gives a handy breakdown of donor cars.

Deck the Walls

www.deckthewalls.com/

The website of the chain of stores offering art work and picture framing.

Friends Reunited

www.friendsreunited.co.uk/

This is a brilliant idea. Visit the site, enter your old school or college and get in touch with friends you used to have at school. Catch up with the gossip and read others' memories of the greatest days of your life.

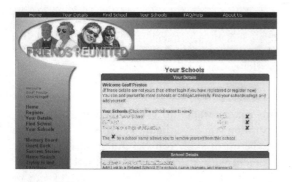

Guitar Tabs

www.guitartabs.net/

Learn to play thousands of popular hits on your guitar by entering the name of a song and downloading the guitar chords. The chord patterns are provided so even if you don't know the chord shape, you can still strum the tune. There are dozens of links to sites offering free tabs.

Kandle Factory, The

www.thekandlefactory.com/

At one time, not very long ago, candles only ever appeared when there was a power cut. Now electricity is more reliable, candles have become commonplace.

MacDonald Fyne Mugs

www.mfa-uk.co.uk/

This company produces personalised mugs, pens, glasses, mouse-mats and a great deal more.

Panoramic Views

www.maitechnology.com/vistarama/earth/

Zoom in on the world map to pick a continent, then a country, then a city and finally a location from the map. On the left will be a scrolling 360° view of the area.

Remote Controls

www.remotecontrols.co.uk/

Remote controls for the TV, video and hi-fi are probably the most abused pieces of electronic equipment we have in our homes. They get dropped, trodden on, lost down the back of the sofa and eventually they work either intermittently or not at all. Buying a multiple 'universal' changer from your high street electrical dealer is not the answer because you need the original remote control to program it. This company can bail you out by matching and supplying a huge range of original remote controls for most leading makes of TV, video and hi-fi.

Red Letter days

www.redletterdays.co.uk/

Visit this site and choose from a range of activities including flying a helicopter, driving a tank or going up in a hot-air balloon.

66. Mobile Phone Accessories

About Cellphones

cellphones.about.com/

This huge site features all the latest news about cellular phones.

Buzz Mobile

www.buzz-mobile.co.uk/

Fun – lots of downloadable ringtones and graphics.

Carphone Warehouse

www.carphonewarehouse.com/

This site provides unbiased advice about buying and using a phone with clear descriptions of the various tariffs and charges.

Just Phones

www.justphones.co.uk/

Buy phones with or without a contract. If you buy a phone without a contract you'll be shocked to find how much it costs.

Mobile Edge

www.mobileedge.co.uk/

More phones and accessories for mobile phones.

Mobile Fun

www.mobilefun.co.uk/

Fun is the word from this superb site featuring some great accessories like flashing keypads and cables to link your phone to your computer.

Mobile Toyz

www.mobiletoyz.co.uk/

Phones and everything for your phone is available from this site.

Mobile Phone Accessories

www.simcards.xpressmarket.com/

Buy phones and accessories online with next day delivery.

Monster Mob

www.monstermob.co.uk/

Another fun site featuring lots of goodies including the latest ringtones and graphics.

67. Mobile Phone Manufacturers

Ericsson

www.ericsson.com/

View the phones and the latest technology at this popular website.

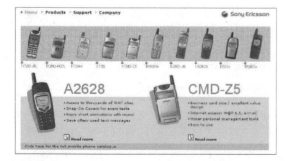

Motorola

www.motorola.com/

Find out about the latest generation phones, as well at what's on the horizon.

Nokia

www.nokia.com/

Apart from full descriptions and specifications of their phones, you can view the accessories and play Snake II – the game featured on many Nokia phones. There is a link to Club Nokia – a site which is also well worth a visit.

Siemens

www.siemens.com/

Another of the major mobile phone manufacturers showcasing its products.

Airfix Models

www.airfix.com/

Many a happy childhood-hour was spent building Airfix kits. In the 1960s a small kit of an aeroplane or car could be bought for 2 shillings (10p) and would take hours to build. If you were really well-off, you could buy a deluxe model costing the equivalent of 17½p. Many of the models available then can still be bought in model shops and online.

Flair Products

www.flairproducts.co.uk/

This company manufactures a range of radio controlled and free-flight model aeroplanes.

Jetex Engineering

www.jetex.org/

Winding up a rubber band powered propeller is fine for some models, but soon you'll want something more. A Jetex engine is a miniature jet engine into which you put a fuel tablet which will give you a few seconds of jet propulsion. It can be used to power model planes, cars, or at a pinch, boats.

Model Flight

www.modelflight.com/

It can be argued that a model aeroplane requires at least as much care in the design phase as the full size version. This website covers everything from a prop size calculator to wing loading charts.

Model Powerboat Association

www.mpba.org.uk/

Everything is here for those who like to spend Sunday mornings at the local duck pond.

North Coast Performance Hobbies

www.ncphobbies.com/

There is a range of models from the past as well as new models including cars, boats, planes and rockets. There's lots of pictures to whet your appetite.

Ripmax

www.ripmax.com/

One of the top radio control model suppliers offers everything for land, sea or air modelling.

Road Race Replicas

www.ho-slotcars.com/

Slot car racing was very popular in the 1960s, but less so 40 years later. This company make their own slot cars on a commercial basis to a scale of 1:64. There are lots of spares and parts to modify models. You can also buy and sell old model cars.

Tamiya

www.tamiya.com/

Apart from the superb range of radio control kits, this company also produce high quality static models.

---

69. Motorbikes

Bikedata

www.bikedata.com/

This site covers all aspects of biking from dealers to training. You can search for new and used machines in the classified section.

British Motorcyclists Federation

www.bmf.co.uk/

If you're a motorcyclist, join this UK group. Full membership details are included on the site, as are the aims and objectives.

BikeNet

www.bikenet.com/

This site features news and views from the world of two wheels and lots of technical advice. There's also a classified section where you can sell or buy a bike.

Bike Trader Interactive

www.biketrader.co.uk/

There are hundreds of bikes on sale on this well-designed website.

Classic & Motorcycle Mechanics

www.classicmechanics.com/

This site covers what is claimed to be the golden age of motorbikes.

Motorcycle Action Group

www.mag-uk.org/

There's plenty of news and comment on this site which is squarely aimed at the biker.

MotorcycleWorld

www.motorcycleworld.co.uk/

The website of one of the top motorcycle magazines featuring news, test reports, classified adverts, and features of general interest.

70. Motorcars

Classic Auto Directory

www.classicdirect.co.uk/

An excellent site for classic car owners and enthusiasts with a database of dealers and forthcoming events. If you would like to buy a classic car, visit this site and look through the classified adverts.

Classic Car Directory

www.classic-car-directory.com/

This well-organised site is essential viewing for classic car owners. You'll find lists of parts suppliers, owners' clubs and meetings.

Global Electric Motorcars

www.gemcar.com/

Petrol cars are approaching the end of their reign, but what will take their place? Electric cars may provide the answer.

Motorcars International

www.motorcars-intl.com/

This is the website of the company that specialises in luxury and performance cars like Rolls Royce and Mercedes Benz.

Motorcar Journal

www.motorcar-journal.com/

A Dutch car magazine offering lots of news and views for motoring enthusiasts.

Owners Club Network

www.ownersclub.net/

A comprehensive list of clubs for the owner to attach him/herself to.

UK Car Owners Clubs

www.ukmotorsport.com/

The directory of owners' clubs can be found by choosing *Single-Make Owners Clubs* from the menu underneath the heading *Tell Me About*. There's a club for almost every car ever made.

Vehicle Maintenance

autorepair.about.com/

Lots of useful help and advice for carrying out all manner of car repairs, from the About.com network.

Woman Motorist

www.womanmotorist.com/

Contrary to popular (male) belief, statistically women are safer drivers. Yes, they have their moments, but not as many as men: particularly young men. This website is for them.

71. Museums

British Museum

www.thebritishmuseum.ac.uk/

London must have more museums per square mile than anywhere else in the world. It seems that whatever subject you choose, London has a museum about it. Curiously, the British Museum seems not to be about Britain. There is an extensive educational section listing programmes and events.

Computer Museum of America

www.computer-museum.org/

The first computers appeared at about the same time as the Volkswagen Beetle. If the car had developed at the same rate as computers, we would now have a car doing over 1000mph (conditions permitting) at a rate of 5,000 miles per gallon, going for 10,000 miles between services and costing about 50p. Trace the development on this website.

Hermitage Museum

www.hermitage.ru/

This museum was founded by Catherine the Great and is generally regarded as the most important museum in St Petersburg, if not in the country.

Imperial War Museum

www.iwm.org.uk/

Apart from the main museum, this site also links to the Cabinet War Rooms, HMS Belfast and Duxford airfield in Cambridgeshire.

London Transport Museum

www.ltmuseum.co.uk/

Now in Covent Garden, the highly acclaimed museum of London's Transport has its own website outlining prices and attractions.

National Motor Museum

www.beaulieu.co.uk/motormuseum

The car collection at Lord Montague's home at Beaulieu is one of the best in the world. Visit this site and see the collection and admission details.

Olympic Museum

www.museum.olympic.org/

This Sydney museum covers the history of the Olympic games from the Greeks to modern times.

Science Museum

www.sciencemuseum.org.uk/

If it's got a wheel or a plug, it's probably here. Petrol-heads and techno-freaks will love it.

Victoria and Albert Museum

www.vam.ac.uk/

A superb museum exhibiting furniture, fashion, silver, and ceramics. Check out this site to find details of special events.

72. Music (fanclubs)

Beatles

www.beatles.com/

The most famous band of all time, although not just a band but a whole culture.

The Carpenters

www.carpenterarts.org/

Until the untimely death of Karen Carpenter, the brother and sister duo were on the top of the world. Karen Carpenter's voice is still unique. You can find out more about them on the site of the Richard and Karen Carpenter Performing Arts Centre.

Elton John

www.eltonjohn.com/

The website of Sir Reg, one of the most enduring pop icons. The site also features inside information from lyrisist Bernie Taupin.

Queen

queen-fip.com/

This superb site features news, registration, e-shop and chat about one of the top groups of the 70's, 80's and 90's. Also features full details of all their records with online ordering.

Roy Wood

www.roywood.co.uk/

Roy Wood was responsible for The Move, ELO and Wizzard. If you've never seen him live, you've really missed something. Visit his site to find out where he's on next.

Simon & Garfunkel

www.sonymusic.com/artists/
simonandgarfunkel/

They were together for only a short time but the music still lives on.

The Rolling Stones

www.stones.com/

Quite simply the greatest rock and roll band in the world.

Status Quo

www.statusquo.co.uk/

The masters of the 12 bar blues, which they have used in every possible variation.

Tina Turner

www.tina-turner.com/

This is the official site of the American rock queen.

101CD

www.101cd.com/

There's a huge range of CDs, vinyl, video and DVD at this store.

BOL

www.bol.com/

A superbly simple ordering facility is available at this store where you can find all your sheet music requirements, as well as CDs and videos.

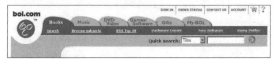

Blockbuster

www.blockbuster.co.uk/

Apart from videos, there's an increasing number of DVDs on sale at this famous high street video library.

CD Paradise

www.cdparadise.com/

There are frequently some amazing offers at this online store which sells more than just CDs.

CD Now

www.cdnow.com/

You'll find lots of music with fast delivery times.

CD-Wow

www.cd-wow.com/

Lots of offers and fast delivery of recorded music.

HMV

www.hmv.com/

One of the oldest music stores famous for the dog and the phonograph logo, although you'll be lucky to find it on the site.

Interactive Music & Video Shop

www.musicshop.com/

Search out the music you want and buy online from this German site.

Internet Music Shop

www.musicsales.co.uk/

Yet more music to search through and buy online.

Jungle.com

www.jungle.com/

A huge, highly publicised online store offering a wide range of recorded music.

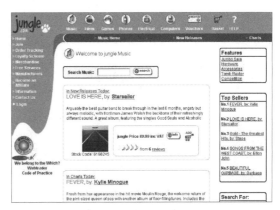

74. Musical instruments

Boosey & Hawkes

www.boosey.com/

The website of the international musical instrument manufacturer and supplier.

Chappell of Bond Street

www.chappellofbondstreet.co.uk/

This is the website of one of the most famous and oldest musical instrument shops.

Gibson

www.gibson.com/

Apart from viewing the superb guitars and downloading music files to demonstrate their sound, you can also buy and sell your quality Gibson guitar using the online auction facility.

Guitar Stop

www.guitarstop.com/

You can buy and sell guitars and find out about guitar lessons at this excellent website.

Macari's Instruments

www.colorsound.co.uk/

This website is as much fun to browse through as the shop in Charing Cross Road, London. It features instruments for sale as well as all the other paraphernalia you need.

Musical Instruments Megastore

www.musicalinstrumentmegastore.co.uk/

Visit this huge store and buy from a massive range of quality and budget instruments.

MusicianShop.com

www.musicianshop.com/

Another top online music store selling instruments and a great deal more.

Smith-Watkins Musical Instruments

www.rsmi.u-net.com/

This is the website of one of the top brass instrument manufacturers.

Yamaha Music

www.yamaha-music.com/

www.yamaha-music.co.uk/

Yamaha build traditional instruments as well as modern electronic ones. This site outlines the full specifications.

75. News

BBC News

www.bbc.co.uk

The BBC News continues to set standards that many others can only try to equal.

CNN Interactive

www.cnn.com/

The website of America's leading news agency.

Journalism UK

www.journalismuk.co.uk/

A website aimed at journalists writing for UK based magazines and newspapers.

Lycos News

news.lycos.de/news/uk/

This Lycos site has stories categorised under the headings Politics, Business and Sport.

News Bytes

www.nbnn.com/

Top stories from around the world bought to you by the Washington Post.

Press Association

www.pa.press.net/

Fast, accurate and impartial news from around the world.

Reuters

www.reuters.com/

The website of the famous news agency.

76. Newspapers

Economist, The

www.economist.co.uk/

Virtually all national and provincial papers now have an online edition. Most of the main features are included in the electronic version.

Electronic Telegraph

www.telegraph.co.uk/

The electronic version of the broadsheet paper features a searchable database to get you to the bits you want quickly.

Guardian and Observer

www.guardianunlimited.co.uk/

The same link will get you connected to both popular UK national daily newspapers.

News of the World

www.newsoftheworld.co.uk/

The famous Sunday paper has similar content in its online version.

NewsDirectory.com

www.newsdirectory.com/news/press/na/

Visit this website to find links to US papers.

Newspaper Directories

usnewspapers.tqn.com/

This About.com site features a rundown of what's in the current US papers.

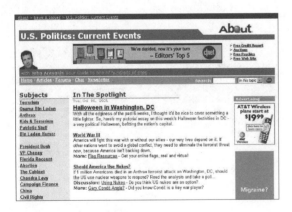

Newspapers.com

www.newspapers.com/

This site provides links to hundreds of newspapers from around the world.

The Times

www.thetimes.co.uk/

Not only current news, but also past news can be found in this electronic version of the famous daily newspaper.

77. Pensions

Pensions Ombudsman

www.pensions-ombudsman.org.uk/

If you have a complaint about your pension, the independent ombudsman can declare a resolution.

Pensionguide

www.pensionguide.gov.uk/

Everything you wanted to know about pensions is covered in this UK site.

Pension Search Directory

search.pbgc.gov/

US visitors can search for any pension owed to them.

UK Pensions Guide

www.ukpensionsguide.co.uk/

Another opportunity to find out more about UK pensions.

Virgin Money

www.virginmoney.com/

www.virginmoney.co.uk/

Check out Sir Richard's stakeholder pensions.

78. Pets

Aquarist.net

www.aquarium.net/

A superb resource for keepers of fish, with information about breeds and a tip of the day. If you're keeping an aquarium, or thinking about starting one, this is a good place to start as it links to sites providing information about plant life as well as which fish to choose.

BirdsUK

www.birdsuk.co.uk/

An informative site for keepers and breeders of our feathered friends.

British Horse Society

www.bhs.org.uk/

If you're lucky enough to have a horse for a pet, visit this site for lots of information about caring and riding.

Cats Online

www.cats.org.uk/

The site of the oldest and largest cat charity in the world.

Complete Hamster Site

www.hamsters.co.uk/

Everything you could possible need to know about these cute little furry creatures.

K-9 Online

www.k-9online.com/

You'll find all sorts of canine information including training tips at this website for dog lovers.

Nature Diet

www.naturediet.co.uk/

We are constantly assessing the quality of the food we eat, why not apply the same notion to what we feed our pets? Look at the ingredients of some pet foods and you find a long list of flavourings and colourings. Nature Diet is simply meat, carrot and rice, a few vitamins and not much else.

PetPlanet

www.petsplanet.co.uk/

This is a superb website for anyone who owns a pet or is thinking of taking on what must be regarded as a significant responsibility.

Pets Direct UK

www.petsdirectuk.com/

This site, which is divided into categories, offers a wide range of products for all pets.

Pet's Pyjamas

www.pets-pyjamas.co.uk/

This site offers a wide range of food and other goodies with the aim of making your pet both healthier and happier.

Royal Society for the Prevention of Cruelty to Animals

www.rspca.org.uk/

The world famous charity outlines its work and its campaigns in their efforts to eradicate cruelty to animals and bring to book those responsible for it.

UK Reptiles Online

www.ukreptiles.com/

If you really must have a reptile as a pet, visit this site first. If you've already got a pet reptile, you should still visit this site, even if it's only to play the arcade game, "Snake".

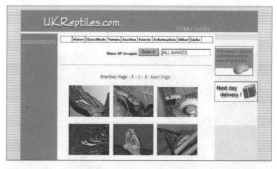

79. Portable Computing

Casio

www.casio.com/

Using a portable version of MS Windows, the Casio organisers are very powerful palmtop devices that easily connect to a desktop computer.

Palm

www.palm.com/

This keyboardless organiser took the world by storm when it was first launched. The tiny device features handwriting recognition enabling you to 'write' directly onto the touch-sensitive screen. It is supplied with lots of on-board software yet is light enough to drop into a shirt pocket. The latest version features a colour screen and a memory card slot.

Psion

www.psion.com/

One of the most popular palmtop computers is the Psion series of organisers. Their ground-breaking designs have proved extremely popular and their size belies their power and ability. Most include a word processor, spreadsheet and database and can link to a variety of external devices like mobile phones to enable the user to send and receive emails.

Rockdirect.com

www.rockdirect.com/

The website of the UK company that sells high quality, high specification laptop computers at very competitive prices. The latest models feature 14" TFT screens.

Beer & Pubs UK

www.blra.co.uk/

Apart from finding out about everything to do with beer and its consumption, you can take a virtual tour of a brewery.

Cool-bars.com

www.cool-bars.com/

Your opportunity to say what you think about bars in London.

Pub Paraphernalia

www.pub-paraphernalia.com/

You can bring the ambiance of your local hostelry into your living room with a range of ashtrays, optics and other hardware.

Pub World

www.pubworld.co.uk/

One of the more interesting features of this site is that you can send someone a virtual drink. You can consume as much of it as you want and still drive home safely and legally.

Pubs.com

www.pubs.com/

There are 100s of traditional ale houses in London. Use this guide to find out more about them.

Virtual Pubs

www.virtualpubs.com/

If you fancy running a pub, check out this site to see what's available.

81. Radio

Capital Gold

www.capitalgold.com/

A superb radio station playing all the old hits with DJs of the era including Tony Blackburn. The songs just get better and better, unlike Blackburn's jokes.

Live Radio on the Internet

www.live-radio.net/

This site links to hundreds of web radio stations.

Media UK

www.mediauk.com/

A comprehensive directory listing radio and TV stations.

Mike's Radio World

www.mikesradioworld.com/

Internet radio is becoming more and more popular and this directory links into hundreds of Internet radio broadcasts from around the world.

NetFM

www.netfm.com/

Apart from listening to the music you can follow the related links to other websites.

NetRadio Network

www.netradio.net/

More Internet radio.

Scottish Internet Radio

www.scottish.internetradio.co.uk/

This Scottish station broadcasts across the Internet as well as in the traditional fashion.

Virgin Radio

www.virginradio.co.uk/

Look at the programme schedule and then listen to the radio online.

82. Religion

Buddhism

buddhism.about.com/

Part of the massive About.com site, this one provides comment about Buddhist issues.

Hinduism

www.hindunet.org/

The official website of the Hindu faith.

Islam and Muslims

www.unn.ac.uk/societies/islamic/

You can search through the Koran on this site and connect to a variety of associated links. There is an outline of the religion and a discussion forum.

Jewish.co.uk

www.jewish.co.uk/

Everything Jewish is covered in this comprehensive site including links to other Jewish sites.

LDS Church

www.lds.org/

The website for followers of the Church of Latter-Day Saints, or Mormons, as they are more commonly known.

Methodist Church

www.methodist.org.uk/

The official site of the non-conformist church founded by Wesley.

Religion

www.hbuk.co.uk/ap/journals/rl/

This site covers a range of issues relating to various religions throughout the world.

Religions of the World

emuseum.mankato.msus.edu/cultural/religion/

This well thought-out website provides an introduction to Animism, Buddhism, Christianity, Hinduism, Islam and Judaism.

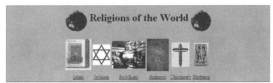

Sikhism

www.sikhs.org/topics.htm

The official Sikh site includes downloadable prayers and a history of the faith.

83. Restaurants

Loch Fyne

www.loch-fyne.com/

We don't eat enough fish in this country. Apart from the odd steak and a couple of vegetarian dishes, Loch Fyne Restaurants serve only fish and other sea foods like lobster, oysters and crab. In keeping with 21st century thinking, Loch Fyne ensures that the environmental impact is at least neutral, and strives to be positive.

5pm.co.uk

www.5pm.co.uk/

Visit this site and book a table in one of the restaurants in London, Glasgow or Edinburgh.

Dine Online

www.dine-online.co.uk/

This site provides independent views on hundreds of restaurants around the UK.

Dine Out

www.dine-out.co.uk/

You can search out a restaurant by location or cuisine.

Eats

www.eats.co.uk/

The database is organised by region and includes hundreds of restaurants, takeaways and cafes. You can read and submit reviews.

Lastminute.com

www.lastminute.com/

If eating out is a last minute decision, visit this site to make a last minute reservation.

Pub Food Guide

www.pubfoodguide.co.uk/

Pub grub varies enormously between outstandingly excellent and outrageously awful. Visit this site to sort out the best from the worst.

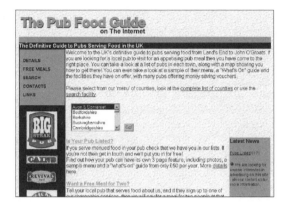

Restaurants.com

www.restaurants.com/

Visit this site, enter a zip code to find a US restaurant.

UK Restaurant Guide

www.taste.co.uk/eatingout/

A superb guide to the UK's best places to eat out, courtesy of Sainsbury's and Carlton TV. Find the top 10 listings for vegetarian, seafood, breakfast and romance.

Virtual Restaurant Guide

www.restaurant-guide.com/

This guide offers a top 20 selection and a large database of restaurant addresses. Browse the map, or search by county, postcode or telephone code.

84. Services

British Gas

www.gas.co.uk/

The website of the main suppliers of gas and related services to residential and business customers. The company now also supplies electricity.

Electricity

www.electricity.com/

A well organised and well designed site featuring news and lots of useful links.

Ofgem

www.ofgem.gov.uk/

The site of the UK gas and electricity watchdog.

Ofwat

www.ofwat.gov.uk/

The site of the UK water watchdog.

VoltNet.com

www.voltnet.com/

Visit this resource with lots of current information and articles of interest relating to electricity.

Water UK

www.water.org.uk/

The website for those wishing to know more about UK's water and sewerage industry. Topics include health, environment, economy and community.

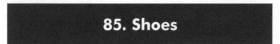

85. Shoes

Adidas

www.adidas.com/

Apart from viewing the current range of sports shoes, there's the chance to see what's coming next. There's also some software to download.

Baby Shoes

www.babyshoes.co.uk/

Baby footwear always looks so cute, especially when you see the same shoe in an adult size. Visit this site and see lots of cute pictures.

Big Shoes Direct

www.bigsize.co.uk/

My son already wears the same size shoes that I do, and compared to some of his mates, he's got small feet. This store stocks a range of shoes for men with large feet, including top-brand trainers.

Hi-Tec Sports UK

www.hi-tecsports.com/

This UK company manufactures a range of sporting shoes. View the collection and check out the technical specifications as well as the impression they're likely to make.

Shoes Direct

www.shoesdirect.co.uk/

Buy shoes online from this UK company with large stocks of top makes including Clarks.

Shoe-Shop.com

www.shoe-shop.com/

All types of footwear are available at this store with secure online ordering.

Shoeworld

www.shoeworld.co.uk/

You can buy online from this site that showcases some of the top European shoe designers.

Vegetarian Shoes

www.vegetarian-shoes.co.uk/

This company offers shoes that contain no animal products, including the glue that holds them together.

Wooden Shoe Factory

www.woodenshoefactory.com/

Clogs are not the exclusive preserve of the Dutch. Visit this site and order a pair of wooden shoes from a variety of styles.

86. Silver Surfers

AgeWorks

www.ageworks.co.uk/

The fastest growing area of computer use is by those who have retired. Having dabbled with computers to a small extent whilst in the latter years of their working life, many over-60s use part of their retirement lump sum to buy their first PC and become Silver Surfers.

Hells Geriatrics

www.hellsgeriatrics.com/

This online magazine specifically aimed at silver surfers provides humour, comment and discussions about a range of issues including political and social issues, and health and sexuality.

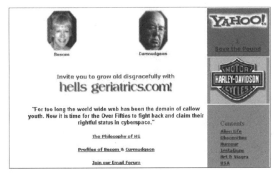

koolsilver.com

www.koolsilver.com/

This superb site invites silver surfers to take an active part in its development.

Silver Surfers

www.silversurfers.uk.com/

A well constructed site claimed to be 'A mature zone for the discerning surfer'. There's lots of interesting areas including a section entitled Discounts.

Silver Surfers

www.silversurfers.net/

Well-constructed directory bought to you by Channel 4 and GMTV. There's lots of links to a variety of sites including entertainment, health and finance.

SilverSurfersClub

www.silversurfersclub.com/

This superb site is laid out like a clubhouse. Move between rooms and find news about achievements, and contribute to the experience.

Technomum

www.technomum.co.uk/

A site for silver surfers by a silver surfer. Find out about outings and pastimes or click on the links to other useful sites.

Download Shop

www.downloadshop.co.uk/

This site offers hundreds of downloads which are paid for when you install.

MS Updates

www.msn.co.uk/computing/downloads

Get all the latest patches and fixes for Microsoft software.

PC Plus Online

www.pcplus.co.uk/downloads.asp

If you missed any of the PC Plus issues, you can get the cover CD software from this site.

Real

www.real.com/

Get the latest version of Real Player and Real Jukebox to enable you to play video clips and sound samples.

Tucows

www.tucows.com/

Lots and lots of downloadable shareware (use it for a short time and pay a small fee if you want to continue using it) and Freeware (absolutely no charge). All software is categorised and can be searched for using the search facilities within the site. A full explanation and star rating is given for each program. In addition to PC software, there's lots of programs for personal organisers like Psion and Palm.

vnunet.com

www.vnunet.com/

Each downloadable application is reviewed and rated. There's some freeware, but mainly shareware.

Xara

www.xara.com/

This company produces top quality software at low prices. There are lots of free downloads including a superb customisable screen saver called Xara Cubes and limited-life trial versions of most of their other products.

ZDNet

www.zdnet.com/

Huge resource of free or cheap downloadable software.

88. Solicitors

Community Legal Service

www.justask.org.uk/

Apart from a directory of solicitors, you can search for legal advice and get advice about applying for legal service funding.

Crown Prosecution Service

www.cps.gov.uk/

Find out what the CPS does and read comments about recent famous or infamous cases.

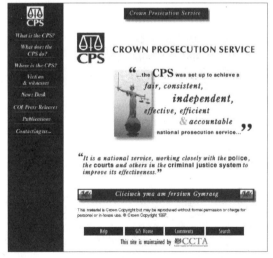

Office for the Supervision of Solicitors

www.lawsociety.org.uk/

If you think you need legal help, visit this site which provides lots of useful help and advice.

Solicitors Index

www.uklegal.com/

This site lists hundreds of solicitors in the UK and provides lots of helpful and useful information.

89. Special Occasions

Anna Bouche Christening Dresses

www.annabouche.com/

This online store offers a variety of colours and styles of christening dresses for girls age 0 to 14.

Bridal Showroom

www.bridalshowroom.com/

As soon as he pops the question, visit this store to select a bridal gown from the dozens of designers showcased here.

Cameras

www.everythingbutthegown.com/

This is a terrific idea. Put a disposable camera on each of the tables and let the guests take pictures during the wedding feast. When you get to this site, scroll down to the menu and choose *Wedding Cameras*. The menu also has lots of other useful links to help make that special day really special.

Century Gift Shop

www.centurygiftshop.com/

Buy collectables and jewellery online from this gift shop with low prices.

GO Greetings

www.gogreet.com/

Visit this site to create personalised greetings cards.

McFadden Farm

www.mcfaddenfarm.com/gifts.html

This company sells organic herbs, garlic braids, and decorative wreaths for special occasions, including corporate events.

Never Forget

www.neverforget.com

Forgetting a special occasion can be a serious offence. To help you remember, visit this site, download the software and get free email reminders of special occasions.

Personal Creations

www.personalize.com/

You can order from a wide range of gift products including quality crystal, and then get the items personalised.

90. Sport

Bike Sport News

www.bikesportnews.com/

Keep abreast of all the latest sporting news on two wheels.

Cricket

www-uk.cricket.org/

There are two teams – one in the clubhouse and one on the field. The team that's on the field is out and they are trying to get those who are in, out. When the team that's out have got out all those who are in, they go in whilst the other team (who are out) try to get those who were in, out. Simple really.

Formula One

www.planet-f1.com/

This is but one of several F1 sites offering news, views, results and interviews with anyone that matters.

Golf

www.igolf.com/

A good walk spoilt.

NASCAR

www.nascar.com/

This is American saloon car racing, usually on oval tracks and at very high speed. Visit the website to keep up to date with the latest stories.

Rugby Football

www.irfb.com/

The game played by 22 men with odd-shaped balls. There's lots of information about the players, the clubs, the matches and the competitions.

Snooker

www.worldsnooker.com/

Snooker was regarded as the sign of a misspent youth. With the introduction of Pot Black on TV in the late 1960s it awakened the general public to the game and the rest, as they say, is history. Snooker was one of the top TV sports in the 1980s.

Sports.com

www.sports.com/

Lots of results and analysis from a variety of sports from around the world.

Sportal

www.sportal.co.uk/

Check out the latest scores and results from around the world as well as news stories.

Sportsweb

sports.onthe.net.nz/

All the sport news from New Zealand is featured in this well-organised site.

Sports Tours Ltd

www.sports-tours.co.uk/

Especially for the football fan, a holiday trip to play football matches abroad.

Tennis

www.tennis.com/

This site features the latest news and views from the world of bat 'n' ball.

BBC Online – What's On

www.bbc.co.uk/schedules/

Visit this site to get information about current and forthcoming programmes and current and future schedules.

Channel 4

www.channel4.com/

Games, chat, schedules and news are just some of the features of this site.

Channel 5

www.channel5.co.uk/

This site lists all the programmes and gives some background information about the channel, forthcoming programmes and the stars.

Discovery

www.discoveryeurope.com/

The science and education channel available to cable and satellite customers provides background information about forthcoming programmes. The site also features information about other Discovery channels such as Wings and Home & Leisure.

EuroTV

www.eurotv.com/

Find out what's on across Europe.

History Channel

www.historychannel.com/

History was never my strong suit, but this channel has some superb documentaries and biographies, many of which can help put the current world situation into context.

Visit this site daily to check out *This Day in History*.

ITV

www.itv.co.uk/

There's lots of information about the UK's independent television company. The menu provides links to top TV programmes where you can find out more about them.

Satellite TV Europe

www.satellite-tv.co.uk/

This is the online version of the published magazine providing news about programmes and background information.

Aiwa

www.aiwa.com/

The website of this consumer electronics manufacturer showcases its latest models.

Grundig

www.grundig.com/

This European manufacturer produces a wide range of TV and video solutions which are detailed on this site.

Hitachi

www.hitachi-consumer-eu.com/

This huge Japanese company produces a range of solutions which can be viewed and compared.

JVC

www.jvc-europe.com/

The Japanese Victor Company, responsible for VHS format, display their latest products.

Panasonic

www.prodcat.panasonic.com/

Another popular brand displaying its wares.

Philips

www.philips.com/

Apart from TV and video, Philips produces a wide range of products from hi-fi to light bulbs for cars.

Samsung

www.samsungusa.com/

Browse through this superb site and see the latest products.

Sony

www.sony.com/

Akio Morita's Sony Corporation probably did more than any other company to dispel the image of Japanese products as being cheap, poor quality imitations of western products. This site showcases their products and provides full technical specifications.

93. Theatre

Aloud.com

www.aloud.com/

Search this site by the name of the venue or by city to find a performance and then book online. Look out for the icon that indicates seats are selling fast.

Cinemark Theatres

www.cinemark.com/

Find out what's on at over 2,000 screens in the US and Canada.

Hot Tickets

www.thisislondon.co.uk/

This locator and online ticket ordering website is part of the London Evening Standard's website.

Official London Theatre Guide

www.officiallondontheatre.co.uk/

Visit this site to find out what's on in London. Search for a performance by name, date or theatre.

Online Tickets USA

www.onlineticketsusa.com/

There are some special deals on certain shows booked online on this website.

UK Theatre Web

www.uktw.co.uk/

Theatrical gossip, and much more.

What's on Stage UK

www.uktw.co.uk/

Find out what's on and book online.

94. Toys

Barbie

www.barbie.com/

The famous doll that most girls seem to own has her own website laid out, appropriately, in candy colours.

Corgi

www.corgi.co.uk/

In the 1980s. these were the models to have. Details include suspension, windows and opening doors or bonnets. Not forgetting jewelled headlights. Many of those early models are now being re-released.

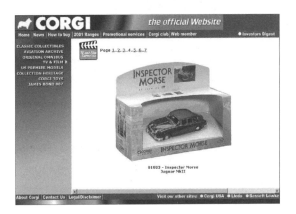

Hasbro

www.hasbro.co.uk/

Visit this site to see the huge catalogue of toys and games.

Hornby Trains

www.hornby.co.uk/

Their website is rather like an extension to their catalogue, with copious pictures of engines and carriages and goods wagons. There is a news page and a very interesting section outlining the history of the company.

Lego

www.lego.com/

This site gives all the information, history and help you'll need. For example, did you know there are over 80 billion Lego bricks in the world today? I wonder who counted them all?

Matchbox

www.matchboxtoys.com/

These small cars used to be sold in a box that resembled a matchbox. Now they make a lot more than just toy cars.

Scalextric

www.scalextric.co.uk/

Scalextric is probably one of the best known slot car systems. The website details the models, the sets and occasionally offers limited-edition cars that cannot be purchased anywhere other than on the Scalextric website.

Teddy Bears

www.teddy.co.uk/

If you go down to the woods today, you're sure of a big surprise. If you go to one of their websites, you're in for another surprise.

95. Train times

Amtrak

www.amtrak.com/

Plan your journey across America on this, the official site of one of the country's leading railroad companies.

Eurostar

www.eurostar.com/

The fastest way of getting from the UK to the continent is using the Channel Tunnel. Check out the prices and the times and book online.

Heathrow Express

www.heathrowexpress.co.uk/

This site provides a complete timetable of the high-speed service between Paddington Station and the busiest airport in the world.

Rail Page Australia

www.railpage.org.au/

Visit the site to get a complete timetable of trains across Australia, and book online.

Railtrack Timetables

www.rail.co.uk/

You can plan your journey around Britain's extensive rail network and sign up to get travel information via your mobile phone.

The Trainline

www.thetrainline.com/

Rather than queuing up at booking offices, visit this comprehensive site and book your train journey in the UK from the comfort of your home.

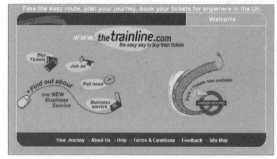

Thetube.com

www.thetube.com/content/journey/

Find your way around London's Underground system with this journey planner.

TrainWeb.com

passengerrail.com/

This site provides a complete guide to train services in the USA and Canada. One interesting feature is a link to a series of webcams that provide a view of sections of the network enabling you to see if there are any problems along your intended route.

VIA Rail Canada

www.viarail.ca/

This site, in both English and French, provides lots of information about train travel in Canada including maps of major destinations, timetables and booking information.

96. Watches

Aviator Watches

www.aviator--watches.diamond.com/

This online shop sells quality watches from top manufacturers at reduced prices. There's also a glossary of terms that's worth investigating. Note the double dash in the URL.

Big Watch Co.

www.bigwatch.procossax.com/

You can shop for quality watches which are categorised by manufacturer. There is also a selection of other quality timepieces.

Breitling

www.breitling.com/

View the quality timepieces designed for pilots and others in the aviation field. There's some interesting information about the technology used to create these fine watches and a directory of retailers.

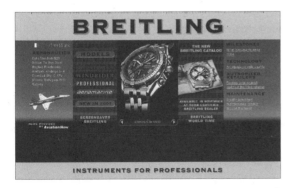

Celtic Watches

www.celtic-watches.com/

This company manufactures watches as well as retailing Celtic, Cairn and Charles Rennie Mackintosh watches.

Gray & Sons

www.grayandsons.com/

This company buys and sells pre-owned watches as well as servicing and restoring watches from top manufacturers.

Kelkoo

uk.kelkoo.com/

If you're looking for a quality watch, visit this site which offers watches at competitive prices.

Omega

www.omega.ch/

The website of the famous Swiss watch maker whose products are worn with pride by celebrities including four times world motor racing champion, Michael Schumacher.

Rolex

www.rolex.com/

The Rolex Oyster is one of the most sought after watches in the world. Visit this superb website and find out all about the watches and the technology behind them.

Seiko Group

www.seiko.com/

This famous watch maker uses a combination of modern and traditional technology to build quality time pieces for all ages and budgets.

Swatch

www.swatch-shop.co.uk/

These fun watches come in hundreds of designs ranging from subtle to startling. See the latest designs and buy online.

TAG Heuer

www.tagheuer.com/

Heuer is one of the oldest Swiss watch makers and this website details the history as well as outlining the products. There is also a directory of authorised dealers.

Tissot

www.t-touch.com/

One of the latest creations from this innovative company is the touch screen watch. Use this site to find out how it works and where to get one.

Watch Company

www.watchco.com/

This online retailer sells fashion watches. Order online and you'll get free carriage in the US.

Watches of Switzerland

www.w-o-s.com/

This is the website of the up-market high street retailer. Apart from showcasing their wares, there are links to manufacturers.

watchnews.com

www.watchnews.com/

If you want to get the latest information about trends in watch design, visit this site.

Watchzone.com

www.watchzone.com/

Visit this site to purchase a watch from one of several manufacturers.

97. Weather

BBC Weather Centre

www.bbc.co.uk/weather/

It's important to know what the weather is doing, especially if you live in a climate known for unpredictable changes. The BBC site provides weather maps and forecasts for all of Great Britain, with satellite and radar details.

CNN – Weather

europe.cnn.com/weather/

The US news agency provides five-day weather forecasts for many major cities throughout the world.

Met. Office

www.meto.gov.uk/

Find out about the science of weather forecasting from the site of the Meteorological Office.

Online Weather

www.onlineweather.com/

You can get detailed weather forecasts for Britain and Ireland, including forecasts for over eighty cities across the UK. There are also some excellent climate charts.

Very Useful UK Weather Page

www.maalla.co.uk/uk-weather/

You can view satellite images and find out the weather forecasts for your area in the UK.

Weather Channel

www.weather.co.uk/

Visit this site and view satellite shots as well as a guide to UK and international weather.

98. Whitegoods

AEG

www.aeg.de/

The website of the manufacturer of quality domestic appliances can be viewed in either German or English.

Bosch UK

www.bosch.co.uk/

This company manufactures a wide range of products including whitegoods. The site showcases all of its products and provides technical details.

General Electric

www.ge.com/ath.htm

View the entire range of whitegoods and locate a local distributor or buy online.

Hotpoint

www.hotpoint.co.uk/

Not only does this company produce a wide range of whitegoods in white, they also produce them in silver, beige and a rather fetching shade called Oyster. Visit the site and see all of the products, in all of the colours with full technical specifications.

Informed Buying

www.informedbuying.com.au/

This Australian site provides independent comparisons of products to help you choose the best one.

Whitegoods

www.whitegoods.co.uk/

This site aims to make the purchase of domestic appliances as simple and painless as possible. There's lots of advice, recommendations and explanations.

Miele

www.miele.com/

This manufacturer of quality domestic appliances showcases its products with full technical specifications.

Woodalls Electrical

www.woodalls.co.uk/

This UK company specialises in quality domestic products. View the products and buy online.

Zanussi

www.zanussi.com/

A major manufacturer of whitegoods showcases its products and provides technical specifications.

99. Youth

Generation Youth Issues

www.generationyouthissues.fsnet.co.uk/

This well presented site aims to challenge young people's views. There's lots of articles to provoke thought on topics including crime, bullying and rights.

Mind, Body & Soul

www.mindbodysoul.gov.uk/

A healthy site, especially for teenagers, covering mental, physical and sexual health. Also includes eating and fitness.

National Assoc. of Youth Orchestras

www.nayo.org.uk/

This site promotes UK Youth bands and provides news, band directory, and concert listings.

Youth 2 Youth

www.youth2youth.co.uk/

Got a problem? Lonely? Bored? Under 23s can talk or email someone about anything.

Youth Against Racism in Europe

www.antifa.net/yre/

The website of the European campaign to halt racism.

Youth Org UK

www.youth.org.uk/

This registered charity aims to develop a virtual community to link and empower young people using the Internet for learning, provide resources, information and advice for young people using the Internet and to support educators working with young people on the Internet.

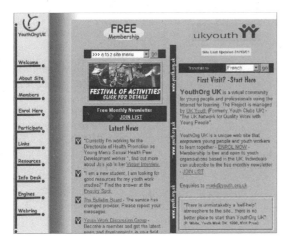

Youth Line

www.youth-line.org.uk/

This website is where young people with problems can mail someone who cares in complete confidence. Emails are always answered within 24 hours and there is a Chatroom which will soon also be monitored 24 hours a day.

Youth Views Online

www.youth-views-online.org.uk/

A site for young people supported by Save the Children Fund. There is a large section on people's rights and several articles of general interest to young people. You can email the staff (who are all in their youth) or join in a chat session online.

100. Zoos

London Zoo

www.londonzoo.co.uk/

Probably the most famous zoo in the world which includes an aquarium, aviary and reptile house, set in Regent's Park, London. Use this site before visiting to check on, amongst other things, the feeding times.

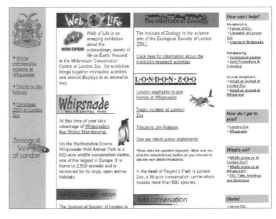

Singapore Zoological Gardens

www.zoo.com.sg/

Pre-plan your visit with the interactive maps and find out what's going at these zoological gardens in East Asia. The site also features interactive games.

Wildlife Conservation Society

www.wcs.org/zoos/

New York boasts five area zoos, a wildlife centre and several aquariums. This site provides directions and includes a calendar of events.

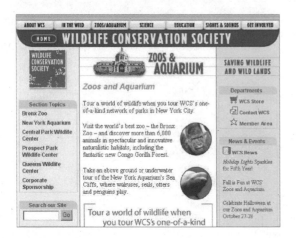

Woodland Park Zoo Seattle

www.zoo.org/

Everything you want to know before a visit is contained in this site including programmes of study for teachers taking school parties.

Zoos, Game Parks, and Wildlife Preserves

www.ohwy.com/wa/z/zoo.htm

This site details several zoos and wildlife preserves in the Washington area of the United States. The site includes lots of superb photographs.

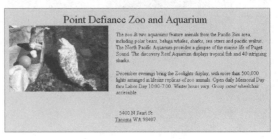